GLOBAL VOICES

Dialogues in International Relations

EDITED BY
James N. Rosenau

with contributions by

James Der Derian

Jean Bethke Elshtain

Steve Smith

Christine Sylvester

Westview Press

BOULDER • SAN FRANCISCO • OXFORD

Copyright © 1993 by Westview Press, Inc.

Published in 1993 in the United States of America by Westview Press, Inc., 5500 Central Avenue, Boulder, Colorado 80301-2877, and in the United Kingdom by Westview Press, 36 Lonsdale Road, Summertown, Oxford OX2 7EW

Library of Congress Cataloging-in-Publication Data
Rosenau, James N.
   Global voices : dialogues in international relations / James N. Rosenau, with contributions by James Der Derian ... [et al.].
      p.   cm.
   Includes bibliographical references.
   ISBN 0-8133-1404-6 (cloth). — ISBN 0-8133-1405-4 (pbk.)
   1. International relations—Philosophy.   2. International relations—Social aspects.   3. International relations—Psychological aspects.   I. Title.
JX1395.R569   1993
327'.01—dc20   93-7933
                                                                          CIP

Printed and bound in the United States of America

   The paper used in this publication meets the requirements
   of the American National Standard for Permanence of Paper
   for Printed Library Materials Z39.48-1984.

10   9   8   7   6   5   4   3   2   1

Global Voices

Contents

Voices

(in order of appearance)

SAR	Senior American Researcher
JUSOFS	Junior U.S. or Foreign Scholar
AFTS	A Former Thoughtful Student
WESTFEM	Western Feminist
TSITSI	Her Third World Alter Ego/Identity
SUKA	Senior U.K. Academic
IRTS	International Relations Theory Scholar
FATHERS (AND SONS) **MOTHER COURAGE** (AND HER CHILDREN) **DOG**	various postmodern personae
SAFS	Senior American Feminist Scholar
SICC	Skeptical Intelligent Concerned Citizen
GORP	Ghost of Realism Past

Prologue

Among the many global voices claiming to depict what moves the course of events, how does one go about selecting the most coherent, the most incisive, the most meaningful? What is the most expeditious way, in short, of comprehending the underpinnings of world politics? These questions have long puzzled and divided observers even during the rare stable moments of history. The dynamics underlying international behavior are so complex that no coherent and shared perspective has emerged to unify analysts. Rather, some have focused on the conduct of states, others on the functioning of economies, still others on the demands of societies—to mention only some of the fault lines along which the divisions get played out. And hovering around the diverse foci of inquiry can be found feminists, realists, globalists, idealists, world-system analysts, transnationalists, postmodernists—to cite only a few of the labels for the different schools of thought and conflicting paradigms, each of which is in turn subject to as many diverse interpretations as there are intellectual, temporal, national, class, and gender perspectives in which to cast them.

But if the large philosophical questions seem central during stable historical periods, their relevance in the present turbulent era of fragmenting states, faltering economies, and restless publics appears all the more compelling. The changes presently unfolding on the world stage are so vast, and the capacity of the extant paradigms to explain them seemingly so limited, that those seeking to comprehend the course of events have become especially sensitive to the need to go back to their theoretical drawing boards for guidance. Such is the purpose of the dialogues presented here. Our goal is to highlight competing ways of approaching world politics through an unusual method of inquiry that, we hope, serves to clarify and join some of the main issues posed by the turbulence that is transforming the global scene.

Our method is that of dialogue, a dramatic form that allows us to emphasize interpretation without concern for the constraints of evidence and to stress raw differences without worrying about nuanced areas of agreement. This is not to imply that we have become alienated from systematic methods of inquiry or that we discount the evidentiary foundations from which sound interpretations must spring. Quite to the contrary, while we differ on the emphasis we attach to various aspects of the knowledge-building process, and while we do not agree on the ways in which knowledge claims ought to be advanced, we share a commitment to the proposition that knowledge cannot cumulate if all evidence is dismissed as irrelevant and arbitrary procedures are used to compile observations. To be dedicated to the tenets of careful inquiry, however, is not to be deprived of the use of a dramatic format. As long as such a format clarifies issues without making irrefutable observations or otherwise implying that reliable truths have been uncovered, then its use violates no basic principle of systematic inquiry. More accurately, as long as the dialogical method is confined to the articulation of conflicting perspectives, then its values need to be assessed in terms of the clarity it brings to issues and not in terms of whether it has yielded any new knowledge.

Stated more positively, with so much in flux in world politics and among those who analyze it, the time seems ripe to give voice to competing perspectives by allowing ourselves the license to posit some of the main voices presently seeking to be heard. It is a license that enables us to get to the core of some central theoretical and epistemological questions without having to note the usual qualifications that add precision but do not alter essential meaning. It is all too easy to be so overwhelmed by the rapidity of the changes transforming the global landscape as to let the core questions slip out of focus, and it is this danger that our dialogues seek to guard against.

Needless to say, our cast of characters is far from complete. Many more voices could have been added to our chorus—Third World analysts, rigorous quantifiers, and political economists are perhaps the most conspicuous silences—but space limitations were such that we preferred to capture at least some of the major perspectives and to acknowledge the omissions rather than to abandon the project. It is our hope that these dialogues will provoke further dialogues that will fill the gaps and expand upon the voices presented here.

Changing Analysts in a Changing World

Our resort to dramatic dialogue also stems from an effort to demonstrate the close and intimate connections between the changes in the structures of world politics and the changes experienced by the observers themselves. Acknowledging these connections is important because they remind us that we can never achieve total objectivity in our scholarship and that we are thus inevitably vulnerable to subtle orientational shifts as the world undergoes profound transformations. Indeed, a distinguished historian suggested that the greater the transformations, the less the subtlety of the change we undergo: "I am not sure that I should envy any historian who could honestly claim to have lived through the earth-shaking events of the past fifty years without some radical modifications of his outlook. ... It is not merely the events that are in flux. The historian himself is in flux."[1]

To be aware of the limits of our objectivity is not, however, to know how these limits operate to orient and bias our analytic judgments. The most noxious version of these links posits them as rooted in one or more of the professional or personal roles we occupy in our daily life. Our national identity offers perhaps the most obvious example of how underlying biases can shape our conceptions of what happens in world politics and why. The inclination to rely on premises and focus on problems that reflect the polity to which we attach our highest loyalties is powerful and ever present. But such loyalties can be served in various ways depending on a wide range of personal and professional values through which national aspirations get filtered. If this was not the case, if national loyalties were the overriding source of professional judgments, then the collective efforts of scholars of the same country would be marked by uniform interpretations rather than conflicting approaches, methodological challenges, paradigmatic diversity, and substantive disputes.

Nor are national identities the only sources of bias that can frame our analyses. Gender, class, occupational, religious, regional, and numerous other affiliations can condition our perceptions of international structures and processes, not to mention the issues to which we attach salience. Thus it is that feminist, developing country, Islamic, Judeo-Christian, business, and Marxist perspectives—to cite only the more conspicuous examples—can be found in the burgeoning literature on world politics. Often, of course, these diverse perspectives overlap and operate as cross-cutting influences on analysts, each of whom occupies numerous roles and is thus exposed to conflicting loyalties and the impulse to synthesize them into a workable paradigm to which he or she is comfortable giving voice.

In assessing how any one of the affiliations may underlie the work of analysts, then, one must be wary of overgeneralizing and take note of deviant as well as central tendencies. There may be, say, underlying national considerations to which most scholars from a particular country are responsive, but their responses may take various forms, and this variety itself might be as much a feature of their collective scholarship as any factors that they have in common.

Of course, stressing the need for caution may unknowingly derive from the biases we have as members of the university setting. Most academics are resistant to the idea that our research is in part a product of national circumstances. Given a self-image in which we see ourselves as autonomous individuals who are accorded tenure for life precisely in order to guarantee our freedom to pursue any ideas and come to any conclusions we like without fear of retribution, it is not easy to admit the presence of subtle and subconscious dynamics that may shape the way in which research problems are chosen, framed, and resolved. We academics pride ourselves on the integrity of our values and the independence of our inquiries; as a result, it is troubling to learn that others see patterns of external influence recurring in our research, patterns that are consistent with the location of our respective countries in the international pecking order.

The possibility of falling prey to pecking-order considerations is perhaps especially troubling for U.S. scholars, many of whom adhere to liberal values that incline them to side with the underprivileged and to see themselves as free of any of the hierarchical presumptions attached to great power status. Critical of numerous policies adopted and pursued by the United States, we are stunned to find that others interpret our work as reflective of an American perspective on the world. After all, some of us reason, our scholarship has focused heavily on the Third World and how its peoples might realize, through political and economic development, better lives for themselves. Indeed, we are quick to note, many of us have been among the most vocal and dedicated critics of the U.S. role in Vietnam, Nicaragua, or Panama. Sure, some of us became policymakers and, sure, others were heavily funded by governmental agencies deeply involved in the Cold War; but those who may have thus given up their autonomy are the exception and do not represent the much larger community of academics who remain ensconced in their universities and who are encouraged to engage in independent inquiry. Furthermore, one need only compare the critical foundations of our work with the noncritical acceptance of public policies by counterparts abroad to appreciate how remarkably independent we have in fact been of pecking-order considerations.

How then can it possibly be argued, we counter in our most resistant moments, that our scholarship is marked by premises and/or foci that might be expected of scholars trained and working under the auspices of a superpower? Easily, respond more and more young colleagues: You haven't the vaguest idea of the large extent to which you and your research are products of your time and your superpower acculturation!

In short, quite aside from the methodological reasons for the dramatic format of the pages that follow, there is at least one emergent dialogue waiting to be joined on substantive grounds. At a high level of abstraction, it is concerned with the nature of international relations (IR) knowledge and its appropriateness to a rapidly changing world in which even the philosophical premises of modernity, which evolved during and since the Enlightenment, are called into question. Its specific focus is the effect of national identity on IR studies in the United States since the end of World War II. For the most part, it is a dialogue across generations that pits those American scholars whose academic careers began with the accession of their country to hegemonic world leadership against those in the United States and abroad who have entered the profession during the more recent period in which the decline in that leadership has accelerated. While some signs of this nascent dialogue have already surfaced,[2] Scene 1 of Act I seeks to bring it more clearly into focus and thereby provoke readers and the other authors into concern about the vulnerability of their research to the course of events.

That the other authors were provoked is self-evident in Acts II through V. Indeed, so provocative were some of the assertions

made by the characters in Act I that the same characters, especially SAR (Senior American Researcher), appear in other scenes
as the target of criticism. It must be emphasized, however, that
each dialogue was separately authored and that the appearance
of the same character in the various acts does not mean that each
of us has participated in the writing of all the dialogues. Rosenau
created SAR's voice in Act I and the Epilogue, for example, but authors of the other dialogues have extended the character and
imagined how SAR might respond in various discussions. Indeed,
it would be a mistake to view the protagonists in each act as necessarily the voice of the act's author. The voices and perspectives
we have ascribed to our characters are composites designed to
serve expository purposes rather than means of expressing our
own viewpoints. Hence our characters are their own selves, created by us but not speaking for us in any literal sense. Our goal is
to uncover conflicting approaches and assessments; it is not to
employ the dialogical method as a means of advancing our own
pet ideas.

The Need for Multiple Scenes

The first four acts were originally written as papers for a panel
at the March 1990 annual meeting of the International Studies
Association in Washington, D.C. At the panel, Jean Bethke
Elshtain became so involved in the discussion of the papers that
we prevailed upon her to write a contribution of her own in the
event the project moved on to a subsequent stage. As it turned
out, a second stage soon became compelling: The panel stirred so
much enthusiasm and controversy that the idea of publishing revised versions of the papers took on a logic of its own. It was a
logic that evoked the immediate support and assistance of an extremely able editor at Westview Press, Jennifer Knerr, whose
imagination and dedication proved central to the transformation
of diverse panel papers into a coherent volume.

Events, however, caught up with the project and necessitated
some revision. The end of the Cold War, the collapse of the Soviet
Union, and the collective military effort to oust Iraq from Kuwait
involved transformations in world politics that were so startling
and thoroughgoing as to challenge the core premises of every

paradigm that purports to explain and trace the dynamics of the field. Or at least it seemed conceivable that some of the central themes of the original dialogues might need to be modified, if not reversed, in the light of intervening events. So a call for script revision went out in the fall of 1992 and, except for Elshtain (who had yet to complete her dialogue), all four of the original panelists extended their papers and added new scenes in which the protagonists encountered each other after the end of the Cold War.

The Pleasures of Drama

Important as the issues addressed by these dialogues are, however, this format has allowed the authors to enjoy pondering them. The context of drama enlivens the mind, lifts the spirit, and engages the emotion, and in the process the writer derives the pleasures of creativity, of knowing that one is moving below the surface and encountering the core of experience and the stark realities within which choices must be made. That is the dynamism that has generated these dialogues, and we urge readers to join in the fun. Cheer or remain silent, applaud your heroes and hiss your villains, get angry or yield to exhilaration—have reactions, in short, that serve to clarify where you are inclined to locate yourself among the global voices clamoring to be heard in a discipline in flux.

James N. Rosenau

ACT I

Superpower Scholars: Sensitive, Submissive, or Self-Deceptive?

James N. Rosenau

Scene 1

A cafeteria on the edge of campus late in the 1980s. It is 9:00 p.m. and the dinner rush is over, leaving just SAR (Senior American Researcher) and JUSOFS (Junior U.S. or Foreign Scholar) at a corner table deeply engrossed in conversation.

SAR: Say, if you want to get into such heady issues, why don't we adjourn to the faculty club? It's comfortable there and we won't be disturbed.

JUSOFS: No, this is fine. These are not issues that call for comfort.

SAR (*seeing he had little choice*): Okay, then why don't you continue? You were saying that I haven't the vaguest idea of what influences have been playing upon me. Do you really mean that? I think of myself as an open, self-conscious sort always on the lookout for extraneous factors that need to be discounted or offset.

JUSOFS: No offense meant; but, yes, that is exactly what I mean. Your work has been creative and insightful on its own terms, but those terms are heavily laden with who you are and who you have been.

SAR: But I go out of my way to be explicit about the criteria of evidence I use, about the reliability of my data, and the reasoning through which I interpret my findings.

1

JUSOFS: I'm not talking about your methodology—at least not yet—I'm referring to your substantive foci, your vision of how the world is structured, your assumptions about progress and its prospects, your notions of what problems need to be addressed. On these matters your research is deeply skewed, distorted, and irrelevant! Even worse, it's dangerous!

SAR (*amused, aware that junior colleagues need room to work out their intellectual identities*): Those are pretty heavy criticisms. I really don't know what you might have in mind.

JUSOFS (*uneasy, aware that senior colleagues can sometimes become overly defensive*): I'm not quite sure how to put it.

SAR: By all means say it directly. How else can I join the dialogue?

JUSOFS: Well, take your notions of progress. For you it's a given that the human condition is bound to improve. You see science as enabling individuals and their collectivities to move the course of events toward a saner world in which people are increasingly free of oppression and poverty. This is the modernist project. It originated with the Enlightenment, but now it has come to an end. It's over! Being totally caught up in the modernist perspective, you can't see that modernism is a cultural artifact, that a postmodern era has begun. It is ...

SAR: Perhaps this makes your point, but I still don't know what you're talking about. Could you be more specific?

JUSOFS: "Ours is the world of the Bhopal and Chernobyl accidents, of the Rainbow Warrior, of Islamic Jihad and the Contras, of AIDS and famine, of Arctic haze, dioxins and the Bruntland report, and of massive flows of displaced persons and refugees in Africa, Latin America and the Middle East without destinations where they would be welcome. Famine threatens millions with starvation and malnourishment while massive surpluses of food pile up in North America and Europe. Governments continue to finance stockpiling of surplus food at the same time that they cut foreign aid and development assistance.

"That, surprisingly, is quite a different picture of the world than the one that is painted by international relations scholarship. These problems are generally recognized by international relations only insofar as they intrude on 'high politics'—the interaction of powerful nation-states. Mainstream international relations paints a particular picture of the world; that of superpower and great power diplomacy, a world on the brink of nuclear confrontation, war-fighting doctrines, defensive strategies of Mutual Assured Destruction, meetings of alliances dedicated to peace through armed force, of interventionism and explosive regional conflicts, summitry of powerful state officials, meetings of OECD [Organization for Economic Cooperation and Development] and its CMEA [Council for Mutual Economic Assistance] counterpart, hazards to the industrial countries' petroleum imports and the strategic plays of military confrontations. In short, international teaching presents us with a world concerned with the global management of interstate power."[1]

SAR (*less amused*): But, of course, we have focused on the management of power. How else do you think the world has gotten through more than four decades without a third world war erupting?! The issue of war and peace, of military strategies designed to deter aggression, is a logical and urgent concern because it occupies the highest place on the global agenda. My guess is that you would be extremely critical if somehow the IR community in the U.S. were to ignore such matters, if we were to ...

JUSOFS: No, you're missing my point. I'm talking about the exclusive preoccupation with the interstate system, which leads to a concern with power management and precludes attention to the many other kinds of crucial issues I mentioned. The truth is that you're so rooted into, so inextricably caught up by, the presumptions of the realist paradigm that global pollution, famines, flows of refugees, and the other issues involving the immediate welfare of people pass readily through your analytic nets. If issues do not involve the power that states seek to wield over each other or the shifting balance of capabilities among them, then you're simply not interested. In effect, your realist paradigm and its neorealist variants are blinders; they hinder your breadth of vision and they ensconce you in a world that, ironically, has little to do with reality.

SAR: That's preposterous! I also have many colleagues who have focused their talents on a whole host of international political economy [IPE] issues, on conflicts and processes that are far removed from war-peace issues. Take the rapid development of the IPE subfield: Its take-off in the mid-1970s paralleled a shift in the editorial commitments of the journal *International Organization*. Just peruse *IO* and tell me that military and diplomatic issues are a prime preoccupation of IR scholars!

JUSOFS: You're not hearing me. I know *IO* well, and I agree it certainly made a substantial intellectual turnaround; yet it too remains hooked into the interstate system. Its many IPE articles start with the presumption that both political and economic issues, and especially the interaction of the two, pose problems and opportunities for the state system. The power being managed may be of a different order, but IPE is still part of the same old premise that managing, steering, or otherwise coping with the global economy is essentially a challenge for the interstate system. I think you'd be hard put, given the way your colleagues probe IPE questions, to see their inquiries in any other context. Now they call it "neorealism," but that is merely a terminological adjustment to emphasize the elevation of economic concerns onto the realist agenda.

SAR: No, the research agenda—note I did not say the realist agenda—has shifted because world politics have changed. The superpowers have moved toward arms control, and security issues have given way to the dilemmas of debt, resource distribution, and …

JUSOFS: So you agree that research agendas follow political agendas. If so, doesn't it also follow that scholars of hegemonic powers adjust their research goals to the interests of the hegemon and that, consequently, they too become hegemonic, that they acquire control—whether they know it or not—over the research agenda of IR scholars everywhere!

SAR (*a bit impatiently*): Is that a statement or a question?

JUSOFS: It's a statement. Let me put it differently. "Realist international relations did not achieve a hegemonic status in the study of international relations until after the Second World War and the emergence of the United States as the dominant global power aiming to reconstruct a world order. Because the United States embarked on a project of forging a world order, the managers of American foreign policy faced the need for knowledge, strategies, techniques, and personnel to pursue the project. The growth of an institutionalized discipline of international relations occurred in this period of growing concern with the large-scale exercise and management of state power internationally. Largely because of the Cold War and the confrontation with the 'great adversary,' the American government funded social science research on a large scale, including the field of international studies. Realist scholarship, with its focus on the problems of great powers, alliances, military strategy and the means to contain challenges to the world order, was able to draw the majority of resources available for research in international politics."[2]

SAR: That's absurd! You're working with a conspiracy theory that just doesn't apply to most of us. Take myself. No one told me during those years to focus on great-power and strategic problems, and I never did. On the contrary, most of what I ...

JUSOFS (*hesitantly, aware of the dangers of over-personalizing*): Wait a minute. Didn't you receive a Ford Foundation International Relations Fellowship in the 1950s so that you could expand and refine your analytic skills?

SAR: Yes, it was 1958.

JUSOFS: And weren't you able to become affiliated with the Princeton Center of International Studies in the 1960s because it had also been funded by Ford and who knows what other agencies? And subsequently, in the 1970s, didn't you receive several National Science Foundation [NSF] grants?

SAR: Yes, those were good years. I was able ...

JUSOFS: And why do you think Ford and the NSF put money into such programs? Was it just to facilitate unfettered scholarship? Or was there some larger purpose?

SAR: I think it was to facilitate scholarship, without any strings attached. Sure, Ford had a mission. The U.S. had become the hegemonic leader and the big question at the time was whether it had the staying power, the will, and the competence to exercise that leadership wisely and on behalf of humane values, or whether it would retreat to its prewar, isolationist orientations. So after the war the foundations put a lot of resources into facilitating the training of people to shoulder the tasks of a newly internationalized United States. I was a beneficiary of those policies, and I suppose I too assumed—though I have no recollection of articulating it to myself—that the world would be better off if the U.S. became a viable, forward-looking superpower, that the global condition was bound to be improved the more solidly we established our capacity to engage in effective leadership on behalf of decent values. But I repeat that no one told me what to study or how to go about it. Indeed, I got the 1958 fellowship in order to tool up in statistics and other social scientific methodologies at Columbia and NYU. I felt I couldn't do the kind of research in comparative foreign policy I wanted to undertake unless I broadened my competence in these directions. And it paid off. I was a coprincipal investigator on several NSF grants because our proposals were judged to be founded on sound scientific criteria and addressed to important problems.

JUSOFS: What kinds of problems?

SAR: In one instance the problem was to design a model for collecting systematic materials on thirty-two countries. It was envisioned as a large data base to be used for Comparative Research on the Events of Nations—CREON we called it—and in the other case we proposed to conduct a survey of the foreign policy belief systems of U.S. leaders. And I might add that both projects yielded valuable findings and, I'm proud to say, they continue to do so.[3]

JUSOFS: But that makes my point. In both cases you put states at the center of the inquiry, and in both cases you presumed that their conduct is the prime determinant of what happens in world politics. The leadership study, in fact, conveys the impression that what the U.S. does, what its leaders believe, constitutes the crucial element in the flow of events. I think it's inescapable that your projects served to advance the hegemony of realism.

SAR (*amused at the simplicity of the argument*): That's news to me. I'll repeat once more, these were projects that I and my colleagues developed on our own. No one told us what to do, and we went out of our way to remain independent of any external direction. Besides, we ...

JUSOFS: I believe you. I'm not saying the hegemonic nature of your research was self-conscious and planned, or even that you were manipulated into doing it. Rather, the premises of realism underlay your training and your success at getting funded. You may not have known it and you may not have intended it, but inevitably your work and the orientations on which it was rested were profoundly hegemonic, both with respect to the IR field and the interests of the U.S.

SAR: Well, that's a line of reasoning I can't break into. Either I unconsciously implemented the goals of unknown elites or I did so knowingly, and there is thus no way you can acknowledge the possibility that I conducted myself autonomously, as an independent investigator free of any impulse to rationalize U.S. conduct abroad.

JUSOFS: Are you saying that there have been no effects of having spent your career under the auspices of a superpower?

SAR: No, I wouldn't say that at all. I find myself increasingly aware of the enormous luxury that attaches to being a scholar in a huge and rich country that commanded the world scene for three postwar decades. But the luxuries that come to mind are not so much the professional mobility, worldwide travel, extensive research support, and other perquisites that accompany wealth and accomplishment. Such perquisites are not trivial. They certainly make life easier and they may even make some of us a bit condescending with respect to the efforts of colleagues abroad. But I'm referring to deeper, more subtle luxuries, a set of freedoms that allow the mind to wander wherever curiosity takes it, to be abstract and theoretical if the impulse to do so surfaces, to remain aloof from the immediate, tough policy problems facing society, and to blithely claim that in the long run society will benefit if a few of its scholars pursue the pure research option that may yield useful bases for assessing short-run dilemmas. The luxuries of hegemonic scholarship, in other words, may be quite the opposite of what you think; they may breed irresponsibility from a societal viewpoint rather than research that justifies and facilitates the hegemon's goals. A lot of our realist colleagues have strenuously claimed as much. They say we have no right engaging in abstract theorizing when the world is coming apart. I suspect that you may feel that way too.

JUSOFS: Is that a question or a statement?

SAR: Just a conclusion based on much experience.

JUSOFS: No matter. You're right! I feel strongly that the luxuries you've enjoyed blinded you to urgent problems. They have stripped you of your critical faculties. They prevented you from abandoning national interest perspectives. Take Vietnam. "It is not by chance that the scholars involved in the protest movement of those years came from so many disciplines and fields of study, but rarely from Political Science and hardly at all from International Relations. It would be wrong to interpret the abstinence of the International Relations Community (concerning Vietnam) as a sign of its greater intellectual maturity and its commitment to a more rational, *realpolitik* understanding as opposed to the emotional idealism of poorly informed and poorly qualified non-experts. It shows, rather, that International Relations had never really been a strictly academic, independent, critical scholarly enterprise."[4]

SAR: The test of such ...

JUSOFS: "And it still is not. It should give us something to think about, how little if at all the enormous losses of lives and the destruction of the social and ecological fabric of a small and distant culture by American power have made an impact on the orientation and the self-conscience of the large community of international relationists. Hardly anybody has seen the need for a critical reassessment of the categories, the paradigms, and the socio-political functions of this particular field of scholarship. Just as in public political consciousness at large, 'Vietnam' has been forgotten. It has been reduced, at best, to another case study for empirical analysis. The search for theory has not been disturbed by it. We/they go on as academically aloof as ever."[5]

SAR: In one sense, you may be right. There is a tendency, I think, in the IR community in the U.S. to focus more on continuities than changes, and in this sense we could probably be more ready to reassess the utility of our conceptual equipment than we are. But you're way off in concluding that Vietnam has had no impact on our theoretical approaches. It underlies, at least in part, the emergence of research on hegemonic decline, on the limits of power, on the constraints of mushrooming interdependence, on the dynamics of cooperation, and on international regimes.[6] It's no accident that these new emphases followed the Vietnam tragedy. What else should we be doing? Would you rather have us spend our time bemoaning and condemning the best and the brightest for having lapsed into being the worst and the dumbest?

JUSOFS: But you yourself have written that it was a mistake for American academics to have been actively and publicly drawn into the political arena over Vietnam. Why, you even made a principle out of being aloof!

SAR: It's true,[7] and I still believe it was a mistake. To get drawn in and take vigorous public positions as a professional is to undermine the profession, to become a partisan, and to be received as any partisan is received—biased, ever ready to distort, to suspend professional judgments on behalf of value goals. If systematic evidence for such judgments is available and widely viewed as reliable, then evoking one's expertise strikes me as imperative. But our field still lacks expertise on such matters, and we're collectively better off acknowledging as much rather than pretending otherwise.

JUSOFS: I'm stunned! I ...

SAR: There's more. By staying professionally aloof we're much better able to engage in the critical assessment you say is so important. In the case of our project on the belief systems of U.S. leaders, for example, we have uncovered substantial evidence of cleavage that has continued ever since the end of the Vietnam conflict in 1975. That is not a trivial finding. Theoretically, it has focused attention on the dynamics of consensus formation and deterioration, not to mention the implications that follow relative to the U.S.'s adjustment to a changing world. So you see, sometimes our so-called "aloofness," our pure research option, does have relevance to immediate problems.

JUSOFS: Yes, and that tells me that the pure research option is no different from the realist who explicitly seeks to enhance hegemonic leadership by being policy-relevant.

SAR: No, you miss the point. The pure research option does not presume what the nature and direction of the short-run benefits will be. I suppose next you're going to tell me that my commitment to science stems from hegemonic sources.

JUSOFS: How did you know? "The realist discipline acquired academic-scientific status with the adoption of positivist epistemology and method in the early 1960s. The emulation of techniques, methodologies and theories of the natural sciences, which had been adopted in the other social sciences, gave international relations the apparent status of a 'science' of interstate relations, further establishing its claim on research resources.

"The positivist focus on generating universal and general theory further reinforced international relation's hegemonic stature and its claim to yield scientific understanding of the dynamic of international 'politics.' The articulation of realist propositions in the form of general laws of international political behavior verifiable by positivist evaluative criteria both set a large research agenda for the discipline and gave it an almost irresistible 'aura' of scientific legitimacy."[8]

SAR (*sitting up, sensing an opening*): You know, you are so very wrong. Those of us who turned to positivist perspectives and scientific methodologies did so precisely because we found realism so wanting. Realists, from Hans Morgenthau to Arnold

Wolfers to Kenneth Waltz,[9] treat the state as a billiard ball and world politics as clashes in which all the balls bounce in the same way in response to the same stimuli. They do not allow for differences among states and they do not allow for the interplay of domestic and foreign policy. Indeed, realism does not even allow for officials being in a quandary, or caught up in bureaucratic conflicts, or intent upon serving class interests, or yielding to idealist aspirations. All officials can do, the realists argue, is act in terms of national interests as these get defined by the power available to them. Morgenthau even went so far as to assert that a policymaker's motives are irrelevant to the study of international relations: "[A]s disinterested observers we understand his thoughts and actions perhaps better than he, the actor on the political scene, does himself."[10]

These premises struck many of us as simplistic, that is, as empirically erroneous, as ignoring too much about the conduct of world affairs, and as opening the door for analysts to parade their intuitive judgments as if they were established facts. So we sought ways of breaking open the billiard balls and of doing so in such a way that our conclusions would be independent of our own intuitions. This insight led us to equate the state with its duly constituted decisionmakers and to attempting to reconstruct the world as the decisionmakers perceived it rather than as we understood it. To do this we needed a methodology for uncovering empirically the central tendencies in the attitudes and behavior of officials. Happily we did not have to look far at the time: The methods of science exactly fitted the need and we enthusiastically adopted them—not as realists seeking to impose a hegemonic methodology, but as empiricists eager to comprehend dynamics in ways that could be verified and tested and verified again.

JUSOFS: But what about neo ...

SAR (*too wound up to be interrupted*): So it's patently false to link realism with science. To repeat, realists in international relations do not practice science. Indeed, they rail against it as much as you do! In their wisdom they are prepared to say that they have keys to understanding that no other approach or methodology can match. Morgenthau spoke of scientific real-

ism, of "objective truth," of "history as it really is," but nowhere
in his writings can one find scientifically framed hypotheses,
much less data appropriate to the testing of his many intriguing assertions. Or read Hedley Bull's blast against scientific inquiry if you think I'm exaggerating the antiscientific biases of
those who approach world politics in terms of an interstate
system.[11]

JUSOFS: I think you ...

SAR (*feeling triumphant*): Wait a minute! Let me finish. I just want
to add that in hearing your argument I hear the realists. Like
them, you probably get apoplectic when confronted with
quantitative analyses and, like them, you seem to feel that your
understanding of world politics is superior to mine. Don't you?

JUSOFS: I only know that realism achieved a hegemonic status and
that it used scientific methods to get there. More specifically,
"positivist criteria of scientific evaluation became tantamount
to 'rules of scholarship' in the field, achieving a privileged status
by which all other work was judged. The domination of method
achieved by positivist evaluative criteria resulted in the insula-
tion of the realist discipline from questioning. As such, outer
limits and parameters were set on what was acceptable
methodologically in international relations 'knowledge.' Similarly, it allowed realism to define the research agenda of international studies. This acted to pre-empt and exclude the formulation of alternative agendas and problems and ongoing
research into them. While there may have been alternative
approaches 'floating' around the margins of international relations, the limited resources available to them and the intellectual hegemony exercised by the realist discipline made the ongoing reproduction of alternative approaches very tenuous
within the context of these ongoing intellectual power relations.
The problematic canons of positivist evaluation and the disciplinary authority structures grounded in them were socialized
into students and young scholars and thereby reproduced.
Through its control of the process of intellectual reproduction,
realist international relations further cemented its hegemony

by turning out the future teachers of international politics, cast in the realist mold."[12]

SAR: Now it is you who are not hearing me! Let me . . .

JUSOFS: Wait a minute. I haven't finished. I'm trying to say that "the hegemony of the realist paradigm became institutionalized through the discipline's authoritative structuring of knowledge production and the establishment of a 'scientific expertise' of international politics. It was within this authority structure that the realist theoreticians set parameters of the acceptable and the 'reasonable' in international relations research, and defined the research agenda. Research and knowledge falling outside of the realist agenda was dismissed as 'unscientific' and not really international relations. The establishment of the dominance of international relations in the field was achieved through its almost exclusive access to research funding, the control and imposition of standards of scientific investigation and the 'licensing of expertise.' This climate left little opportunity for the development of careers and research opportunities outside of realist international relations."[13]

SAR: That's too simple. Perhaps it describes a small portion of the IR community in the 1950s and 1960s, but it certainly doesn't describe the community that I knew. My sharpest recollections involve an uphill struggle on behalf of science, a struggle in which we were subjected to much ridicule over our commitment to quantification and our aspiration to develop broad-gauged theory. We had to put up with endless denunciations and devote valuable time to warding them off. One beleaguered colleague found it necessary to issue "a plea for pluralism in our approaches to international relations, for focused criticism rather than broadside blasts, and for a higher level of mutual respect and reasoned dialogue."[14]

JUSOFS: Let me say about broad-gauged theory ...

SAR: Hold on. I'm trying to give you a feel for what it was like to be one of those IR scholars you say controlled the field's research agenda and insured our dominance by reproducing ourselves through our teaching. You're wrong, just plain wrong. Those of us who adopted scientific methods and goals were a distinct minority. The mainstream, ever concerned about policy relevance, tended to see us as threats, as potentially revealing their intuitions to be unfounded, and they treated us with derision, as naive to believe that central tendencies could be teased out of great amounts of data. And our students tended to drift off, concerned that we neither sought nor claimed a competence to develop theories that could be applied to specific, immediate situations. They wanted relevance irrespective of how it was generated and whether it was grounded in solid research findings. Sure, a few students "saw the light" and stayed on, but the size of subsequent generations was relatively small, even infinitesimal, certainly not enough to insure the intellectual reproduction of which you speak. Indeed, that reproduction has virtually come to an end now. Like you, the funding agencies are quick to dismiss anything that smacks of broad theory, hypothesis testing, and scientific commitment. They want immediate results and are unwilling to gamble on the rich payoffs that broad theory may yield.

JUSOFS (*sighing, sensing that his argument is falling on deaf ears*): Your belief in the potential of broad theory is also part of the problem. I regard it as "the Grand Lie of American International Relations: the seductive search for a theory that can qualify as 'scientific' by positivistic standards, a theory above and aloof from history and political economy, a theory for the relations between state actors at any time and any place, irrespective of the size, dimension, ideological position of given states in the international system. It has led to the production of a set of categories, paradigms and parameters which make the United States as *the* world power disappear behind the smoke screen of a seemingly scholarly and objective academic language."[15]

SAR (*sighing, sensing that his argument is falling on deaf ears*): No, we did not develop what you call "categories" in order to stay aloof from considerations of size, dimension, ideological position, and the other distinguishing features of states; rather, we framed these categories precisely to take account of such variables. I myself wrote a long piece differentiating states by such characteristics.[16] It ...

JUSOFS (*speaking softly, resigned to not being heard*): "I call this search for a general theory 'seductive' because it plays upon the hidden dream of discovering, eventually, some law equivalent to the law of gravity, some formula similar to Einstein's theory of relativity. It is the dream of a value-free discipline, modelled after the natural sciences and not forced to come to terms, critically, with the unique and frightening accumulation of power in conjunction with the world mission of the United States of America. That central problem and concern of most non-American scholars and observers is related to the realm of opinion, but is not part of the work of scholars in the field of IR theory."[17]

SAR (*in a lowered voice, also resigned to not being heard*): Perhaps I'm still seduced, but I don't see why you haven't treated the conjunction of U.S. goals and power as a series of hypotheses, even a theory—call it a hegemonic theory if you like—to be subjected to scientific investigation. How about that? How about playing my game? Why don't you use science, exploit it, see whether it doesn't yield results that conform to your convictions and thereby strengthen your confidence in those convictions?

JUSOFS: I couldn't do that.

SAR: Why not?

JUSOFS: Because I would commit your fallacies. "What is largely absent in American International Relations theory is the realization that such theory has to be historical; not in the sense of ... hypothesis testing based on historical data, but in the sense of a historical understanding and conceptualization of the international system and of the emergence of the US as a hegemonic power, as *the* hegemonic power today. There is no neat formula for this and the search for it is bound to fail. But a theory based upon history, working with historical categories (not historical data), interpreting the structures of the present in the light of the past requires also a creative incorporation and learning from the thinking about politics on the part of the great political philosophers of the past as our contemporaries. By acting as if nobody has ever seriously and systematically thought about the great problems of conflict and co-operation, of war and peace, of wealth and deprivation, of order and justice in the relations between societies and states, the Theory of International Relations is impoverished and becomes reduced to research techniques void of content and perspective. It becomes blind to the rich intellectual and analytical heritage not only of our Western past but of other cultures as well. The result is a tendency to identify International Relations Theory with the rationalization and legitimation of US power and interests. It contributes to the destruction of this discipline as an intellectually stimulating enterprise, undermines its problem-solving function and its role as a critical instrument of change for a better world."[18]

SAR: That is such raw prejudice! There may be some work undertaken by my age-cohorts that is all technique and void of content and perspective, but their work pales in comparison to the studies that use innovative techniques to cut deep into the heart of substantive problems. And I do not know of any among us who dismiss the great philosophers. On the contrary, we seek ideas wherever they can be found; at the same time, we refuse to treat ideas as established facts and, instead, frame them as hypotheses that have to be tested in the context of the present. I suppose that thought is offensive to you, so I'll not pursue it. But let me ask you this: If you admit that "there is no neat formula" for theory building and that your own methods of doing it are "bound to fail," why do you object to our mode of theorizing?

JUSOFS: Based on "the purpose of scientific knowledge as a problem-solving social activity, International Relations as practiced in the US is largely a misdirected failure. It is certainly not responsible for the 'clear and present danger' the US presents today in the international arena, but it shares a good deal of the responsibility by not contributing to a critical perspective, transcending the present in the emancipatory tradition and through the truth-seeking function of academia."[19]

SAR (*staring*): I can't make you out. At first your comments were those of the postmodernist; then I heard the New Left; and now you speak of a critical perspective. Which is it? Those approaches are not consistent with each other, you know, and yet you seem to have no difficulty giving voice to all three.

JUSOFS (*staring back*): All three share in a rejection of your quasi-scientific (and I think realist) orientations. Whether it's called logocentric or just plain bourgeois, your approach is still the dominant approach. It's still imposed on the field by mainstream IR types in the U.S.

SAR (*thoughtfully*): I wonder whether you're opposed to my intellectual perspectives and arguments, or whether you're just flailing out at the authority I represent for you? You seem to be quite capable of finding fault with what we do in the so-called mainstream, but the central thrusts and premises of your alternative models are far from clear. I gather you would focus on the Third World and on the great problems of poverty and justice and famine, but you're essentially silent on war-peace questions, on the nature of international institutions, and on what constitute the prime dynamics of world politics. If the mainstream has gone off course, then tell us how to get back on course, conceptually and theoretically as well as in terms of the values to be examined. Negative feedback is perhaps the most precious of commodities, and you're serving us well in this regard. For that I'm personally grateful. Now why don't you move on to the next step and offer constructive suggestions?

JUSOFS (*less thoughtfully*): You're trying to ...

SAR: One other point. If it's true that we conduct ourselves hegemonically, would it be fair to say that your conduct is that of the rebellious but dependent actor who endlessly seeks new ways of breaking the hegemon's grip?

JUSOFS: That's unfair! You're trying to evade my criticisms. My several voices may be contradictory, but you ...

SAR: Well, all three of your voices seem to be criticizing us for not being like you, just as we tend to be dubious about you for not being like us—all of which affirms the central thesis of this symposium that we are a product of our times and circumstances. (*A waiter clears their table, coughing impatiently.*) I guess they're closing. Do you want to continue the discussion?

JUSOFS: Sure, there's lots more to talk about. But everything's closed now at this late hour. I guess time got away from us.

SAR: We could adjourn to the faculty club. They're open quite late. The chairs are soft, and there's a fire in the fireplace. It's quite relaxing, but ... (*in an ironic tone*) but maybe it would be too comfortable for you.

JUSOFS: I guess we haven't any choice. It's got to do with structure. As I've been saying, yours is the only game in town!

Scene 2

It is the early 1990s and SAR is in his office reading. The phone rings. AFTS (A Former Thoughtful Student) in an urgent voice, is on the line.

SAR: SAR speaking.

AFTS (*from off stage*): You may not remember me. I was in your introductory IR class more than ten years ago. I still remember it, and in recent months I've thought a lot about you.

SAR (*interrupting*): Sure, I remember you, AFTS. You wrote that great paper on IR theory. What have you been doing all these years?

AFTS : A lot of different things. I'll tell you about them some time. But I'm calling because I've been wondering about how you felt about all those theories you taught us in the light of the recent changes in world politics. First, there was the tearing down of the Berlin Wall, followed by the collapse of communism, and then came the Gulf War. How have all these huge changes affected your thinking about IR? Or haven't they?

(*JUSOFS knocks and enters; SAR waves cordially and motions for him to have a seat.*)

SAR: I'm afraid I can't talk now, AFTS, Professor JUSOFS has just arrived, and it's been a long time since I last spoke with him. I'll call you back later. (*pause*) Good. Sure, I'll tell him. Bye for now. (*He hangs up and turns to JUSOFS.*) What a surprise! It's been so long I thought you must have resigned and sought a position abroad.

JUSOFS: No, I had a grant and took a year off. But I've often thought about our conversation that night.

SAR: So have I. There's been such a spate of books and articles on critical and postmodern approaches to IR that I imagined you as feeling vindicated.

JUSOFS: Let's say, satisfied. These challenges do seem to be gathering steam,[20] and the limits of realism and its variants have been further revealed by the upheavals in Eastern Europe and elsewhere.

SAR: Yes, but the Gulf War revealed that realist principles are still vitally alive!

JUSOFS: How's that?

SAR: Saddam Hussein invaded Kuwait, and that provoked thirty-two nation-states to form a coalition to drive his forces out. From a realist perspective, that's classic behavior!

JUSOFS: But I thought you claimed to be an adherent of scientific approaches, that you don't subscribe to the tenets of realism.

SAR: Your recollection is correct. But it could be readily argued that the Gulf War fits well into the realist paradigm.

JUSOFS: Do you argue that?

SAR: No, I don't. I think the war revealed the growing weakness of states and the emergent significance of transnational actors. The necessity of forming a thirty-two-nation coalition and the subsequent reliance on the UN to protect the Kurds, implement the cease-fire terms, and search out and destroy Iraq's nuclear capabilities are hardly expressive of the realist paradigm.

JUSOFS: Hey, SAR, do you realize we just converged around the same thought?

SAR: God forbid! What is that?

JUSOFS: We agree that realism is increasingly inappropriate as an explanatory scheme!

SAR: Yes, but that can also be said about all the other schemes. Critical and postmodernist approaches may be gathering steam, but that's not to say they offer incisive explanations! Take your New Left voice, for example. The turbulence of world politics has also uprooted Leninist perspectives.

JUSOFS: Perhaps, but the post-Marxist notion that structures are socially constructed—fashioned out of the intersubjectivity of elites and publics—has certainly been upheld by the course of events. The Cold War, it turns out, consisted of socially constructed structures, and that's why it collapsed so quickly and so dramatically: Once people saw through the premises and habits on which the Cold War thrived, the whole system came apart.

SAR: It's my impression that postmodernists, critical theorists, and Marxists were no more prescient about the collapse of the postwar order than those of us in the IR mainstream. All of us have been overwhelmed by the pace of change, isn't that right?

JUSOFS: I suppose so.

SAR: So you'd agree that we all have to go back to the drawing board?

JUSOFS: I guess I do. But I imagine it will be especially hard for you to do that.

SAR: Why?

JUSOFS: Because you attach so much weight to being a super-power scholar, and now your country is no longer the super-power it once seemed to be. If Washington is in disarray over being irrelevant to the course of events—over being on the sidelines while historic developments unfold—you must also be disoriented. Now you're a *former* superpower scholar, and I'd guess that leaves you at something of a loss.

SAR: In what sense?

JUSOFS: You spoke of the "luxuries of hegemonic scholarship," of being able to "remain aloof," and of being able to "pursue the pure research option." I assume that those psychic luxuries are no longer available to you, that now you feel the pull of current problems, else your irrelevance and irresponsibility will be all the more conspicuous!

SAR: We still have our empirical methods, and more than a few of us have used them to trace and assess the extent of hegemonic decline.[21]

JUSOFS: And more than a few of you have been intent on demonstrating that such a decline has not occurred.[22]

SAR: You see, we're still vitally alive to the larger meaning of events and alternative interpretations of them. ... (*pause by way of changing the subject*) I have to get going, but first, tell me, how did you fund your year off?

JUSOFS: If I told you that, you'd have the last laugh.

SAR: No, my friend, I'd be pleased that we're converging around common practices. ... (*pauses again*) By the way, that was AFTS on the phone when you arrived. He asked to be remembered to you. He's not ready to settle for the idea that we have to return to our theoretical drawing boards. He specifically wanted to know what the end of the Cold War and the Gulf War have done to my IR theories.

JUSOFS (*after a moment of silence*): Well, what's the answer? What have they done to your thinking about our field? Now that you're no longer a superpower scholar, will you have to readjust your theories when you get back to your drawing board? Or are they still intact?

SAR (*thoughtfully*): I feel humble mostly, but in some ways I also feel vindicated ... uh, what you call satisfied.

JUSOFS: That's contradictory. How can one be both a loser and a winner? Face it, SAR, your theories have been upended. They're beyond redemption. They're the voice of a loser!

SAR: No, JUSOFS, you're missing a couple of key points. I grant world politics have undergone a breathtaking transformation.

That the breakup of the Soviet empire following the failed coup occurred in less than three weeks is staggering, just as earlier the quick end of the Cold War left everyone speechless. So there are good reasons to feel humble, to pause and ask how so much could transpire that seemed unimaginable only a short time ago. I've been in the field for a long time and had thought I was immune to being surprised.

JUSOFS: Isn't that the point?! Can't we say that unanticipated and surprising outcomes are the only regularity, that every moment of history is different and thus ever capable of turning in unexpected directions!

SAR: Now you're surprising me, JUSOFS. It wasn't long ago that you were expressing certainty about the Cold War and its sources. I recall you saying that …

JUSOFS: No, don't do that to me. I told you U.S. policy was misguided, and events have proven me right! Look at all the Iraqi soldiers we murdered for no good reason!

SAR: Hey, how about a little humility on your part, JUSOFS? Haven't you also learned from all these startling events? Can't you admit to bewilderment, or at least awe, over the scale of the changes? Can't you pause and ponder, suspending firm conclusions until you've thought through the implications of a world without a Cold War and a Soviet empire?

JUSOFS (*momentarily startled*): Why … I mean … I … That's pretty damned pompous, SAR, and you haven't even said why you feel vindicated. If your humility leads you to a holier-than-thou perspective, your sense of vindication will probably reach new heights of pomposity!

SAR: Call it what you will, but I feel vindicated because I've always argued that as theoreticians we must remain deeply committed to probabilistic forms of analysis, to allowing our variables to vary fully across any continuum from high likelihoods to extreme improbabilities, and that in this way we can never be fully surprised by what happens.

JUSOFS: Are you about to reverse yourself and say you weren't surprised by the collapse of the Soviet Union, that you allowed the coherence variable to vary to the point of total disintegration?

SAR: I suppose it would sound pompous if I said that I wasn't surprised and that I anticipated what happened. But in fact I did allow for it, even though I was stunned by the suddenness and speed of the USSR's demise following the failed coup.

JUSOFS (*cautiously*): Aren't you being a bit evasive? How can one allow for an outcome without predicting it?

SAR: For years I told my students that I couldn't discern any underlying values shared by the diverse peoples of the Soviet Union. I kept saying that only the authoritarian rule of the Communist party held the system together. At the same time, it has always seemed crucial to me that we approach any social or political system as endlessly on the verge of collapse. So it was not surprising that the Soviet Union disintegrated once the party lost its controls. I didn't predict the timing or the exact form of the disintegration, but I did allow for it.

JUSOFS: That's pretty vague. Have you ever been more precise about this verge-of-collapse business?

SAR: Sure, I've even proposed in print that it is an awesome accomplishment each time a system gets from Monday to Tuesday, that moving through time intact does not occur automatically, that forces are always at work in any system that would, if possible, configure it differently on Tuesday.[23]

JUSOFS: That's still nothing more than a vast generalization. I bet you've never applied it to a specific situation in advance!

SAR: Oh yes I have! Before Gorbachev, before Chernobyl, when nothing seemed more stable than the Soviet Union, I argued that the systems-are-always-on-the-verge-of-collapse approach required us to place Kiev and Beirut on the same continuum and to allow for the possibility that even Kiev could experience a shift from stable tranquility to restless turmoil.[24] Tell me, JUSOFS, have you had occasion to observe the political scene in Kiev lately?

JUSOFS (*hesitantly, a bit chagrined*): Well, uh, no, I haven't.

SAR (*having a hard time containing his sense of triumph*): I suggest you do.

JUSOFS: I will. (*pauses, unwilling to concede an insight*) But so what?! Granted your approach allows for systemic collapse, but does it anticipate what happens next? Can you derive a scenario for the coming years in the former Soviet Union and for the emergent global system?

SAR: Only in the most general way. I've posited the centralizing and decentralizing tendencies at work in world politics as ensconced in endless tension, as so intertwined as to foster a cyclical process in which the predominance of one set fosters the resurgence of the other.[25] This is why the collapse of the Soviet Union was quickly followed by efforts to preserve a modicum of union that would serve the centralizing needs of all the republics. I'd guess these tensions will continue to cycle back and forth for years to come—certainly through my lifetime and probably through yours, JUSOFS.

JUSOFS: That's such a broad statement as to be almost meaningless!

SAR: Can you do any better, JUSOFS?

JUSOFS (*looks at his watch*): Let me think about it. I should be going. You said you'd call AFTS back, and I wouldn't want to prevent him from hearing about the tensions between centralizing and decentralizing tendencies. (*He laughs as he moves toward the door.*) I'm sure he'll be impressed with ... with your theory!

SAR: You think it's a lot of gibberish, don't you, JUSOFS?

JUSOFS: As a matter of fact, I do. We should be able to do better than that!

SAR: Are you saying we should have more cogent theories?

JUSOFS (*awkwardly*): Well, yes, that's what I'm saying.

SAR: And that they should allow for greater variance in the key variables?

JUSOFS (*even more awkwardly as he opens the door to leave*): I guess so.

SAR (*as he starts dialing AFTS*): You're beginning to sound like a good probabilist. I'm glad we've come upon an area of agreement between us.

(*JUSOFS, annoyed, starts to go back into the room to argue, but it is too late, so he waves good-bye and leaves.*)

SAR (*into the phone*): It's me, AFTS, I'm returning your call. Now what was it? ... Oh yes, you want to talk about what the world is doing to our theories. ...

The final curtain closes as SAR pulls his chair into the desk, plants his elbows firmly on his papers, nestles the phone into his neck, and conveys the impression of settling into a long conversation.

ACT II

Reconstituting a Gender-Eclipsed Dialogue

Christine Sylvester

In a wide variety of cultures and discourses, men tend to be seen as free from or as not determined by gender relations. Thus, for example, academics do not explicitly study the psychology of men or men's history. Male academics do not worry about how being men may distort their intellectual work, while women who study gender relations are considered suspect (of triviality, if not bias). Only recently have scholars begun to consider the possibility that there may be at least three histories in every culture—"his," "hers," and "ours." "His" and "ours" are generally assumed to be equivalents.

—Jane Flax[1]

Dear Westfem,

I am writing to invite you to participate in a dialogue on how national factors may impinge on international relations studies. As you know, I have begun such a dialogue with JUSOFS and, although our talks are fascinating and often a bit combative, I'm not sure either of us has succeeded in persuading the other to admit to inadequacies, our brilliant ripostes notwithstanding. Surely the process will be enlivened by contributions from a variety of perspectives.

Sincerely,

SAR

Dear SAR,

Thank you for the invitation to join your latest dialogue. Obviously you know that my contributions to a discussion of national factors and identities will reflect a variety of feminist perspectives on IR as a field of theory and practice. I welcome this conversation because context—national or otherwise—looms large in feminist discussions of differences between men and women, among women, and between feminist and mainstream understandings of IR. For the very reason of difference, may I suggest that we entertain another woman's voice in the dialogue, one whose context is different-similar-hyphenating to mine.

I hope the addition will meet with mutual approval. I am very aware that the mainstream of IR is reluctant to include feminist interpretations within the field, the odd conference here and there on feminist IR notwithstanding. The silent treatment we "alternatives" receive surely isn't because feminist thinking is new, irrelevant to IR, inaccessible, or nonprogressive. The pre-1990 work of Jean Elshtain, Cynthia Enloe, Sara Ruddick, Maria Mies, Sharon MacDonald, Patricia Holdern, and Shirley Ardener, and the material on women and development, all reveal myriad points of intervention in IR theory by feminist-minded scholars.[2] Yet if you look at Yosef Lapid's 1989 review of controversies in the field, you will find that it is absolutely devoid of reference to feminist concerns, a trend we saw in earlier such reviews.[3] When feminists consider the certain gender affirmations and certain gender silences that scream unnoticed throughout the pages of most undergraduate textbooks on international relations, "our" astonishment is difficult to contain.

In your synopsis of the first dialogue with JUSOFS, you said that people like yourself had to struggle to batter down the Berlin Wall of realism to get science into IR—"a struggle in which we were subjected to much ridicule over our commitment to quantification and our aspiration to develop broad-gauged theory."[4] What strikes me, however, is how quickly you succeeded in gaining an audience and a measure of respectability for your "alternative" project. Feminist theorists have already been struggling a decade longer than you did, and we are still treated like bright but quaintly misguided and undisciplined thinkers by IR insiders. There is obviously some crucial difference between arguing for science in IR and arguing for conscious recognition of the gender blinders of the field. What factors make the one more quickly respectable than the other?

Maybe we can expand the spaces around "national factors" so that this and other feminist-driven concerns can march rather than creep into our discussions of IR studies.

Sincerely,

Westfem

Dear Alteri Identia,

From my vantage point in Harare the world seems excitingly mad. South Africa, as you know, seems to be changing at last, and some of my colleagues are already talking about a future SADCC [Southern African Development Coordination Conference] that will include rather than work to isolate South Africa in the region. A new era of coalition politics appeared to be dawning in Angola after fifteen years of civil war and, of course, Namibia is now technically free of South African rule. Hard to believe, eh? Indeed, how many of these changes can we feminists believe?

The momentous events in Eastern Europe had all of us running this way and that. Our ruling party [Zimbabwe African National Union–Patriotic Front] took the hard line at first, what we call the Cuban line, against perestroika in the Soviet Union and the breakup of democratic centralism in the GDR and Czechoslovakia. It said that socialism was too important to be subsumed within bourgeois notions of free-market democracy. Then it bowed to the "democratization" line sweeping Eastern Europe—and the USSR itself—and said there would not be single-party rule in Zimbabwe in the near future. The people here were happy.

Ah, but will "the people" everywhere become pawns in the shifting meanings of democratization? We now see that the GDR's democratization drive was wholly subsumed by the forces of "merger." Democratizing students of Tiananmen Square were sacrificed in China to "unity." In Yugoslavia, democracy brought a horrible civil war. Here in Harare, the police still periodically round up "law-dissenting" prostitutes, invariably making the "mistake" of gathering up a few urban women going home from the office. So we have street democracy for men but not for women. Also, we watch the government discipline our university so that student protests cannot rule the spaces of intellectual development. It seems that parameters of legitimate voice—of tolerance for diversity—narrow even as we proclaim the era of global democracy.

Frankly, I worry about women getting lost or crushed by the invisible

*sjamboks of "democracy."[5] Remember that lecture you and I attended
years ago by the feminist historian Joan Kelly? It was entitled, after her
writings: "Did Women Have a Renaissance?"[6] At the time I almost didn't
attend because I was sick of learning history through the eyes of westerners. You dragged me there, remember? All the while I grumbled. Well, I
think about that lecture now and wonder: Has Zimbabwe—this "progressive" country of racial tolerance, this economic and social Pride of
Africa—been progressive for women or mostly for men?*

*Right after our anticolonial war, we used to hear about the valiant
women comrades who had carried babies on their backs and AK-47's
over their shoulders as they fought Rhodesian rule alongside the valiant
guerrilla men. Now we hear how disruptive the new emphasis on wom-
en's rights has been to traditional values. How did our wartime contributions come to be denigrated as a threat to society? Did we unwittingly
stand by while her-stories about the struggle for Zimbabwe were subjugated in a his-storical account of liberation struggle? Were we too ac-
cepting of postindependence ideologies and policies crafted mostly by
our brave men to push for more spaces for ourselves?[7]*

*Look around the world. Once again, the leadership for democracy
comes in male bodies. Will we hear from women in the "new" world order, or will we continue to be bombed in wars planned by some men to
"get" other men—that Persian Gulf War being just another in a chain of
such outrages?*

*Westfem-self, I tell you, we women have been gagged by tradition and
colonialism for so long that now it is difficult for us to insist on our
voices, ideologies, and statecrafts. We speak, nonetheless, and it is ironic
that just when the center of gravity in the world is shifting from two
superpowers to "unimportant" nations, from single voices claiming to
speak on behalf of the world, let alone "their" people, to multiple voices,
"our" governments are extolling the virtues of their own voices, which, of
course, are the voices of masculine privilege in our societies. A woman
defeats Daniel Ortega in Nicaragua. Should we be pleased or in mourn-
ing for the Sandinistas? Margaret Thatcher passes from the political
scene in Great Britain. Is this a monumental passing or a passing of the
baton to people who stand once again for women-eclipsing democracy?*

*This is all so important that I could go on and on. Maybe I can go on
and on at the one-day conference on national factors and international
relations studies. Perhaps the presence of a third-world-woman-first-*

*world-feminist will help get us away from the narrow concerns of super-
power men and on to some truly weighty topics.*

Pamberi,

Tsitsi

Dear Westfem,

*I have just learned that you and I will be participating with SAR in a
new dialogue on national factors in international relations scholarship.
I am happy to attend, of course, and find it amusing that he invited
both of us, for I doubt your perspective will be much different from
mine; you know I heartily agree that dissident voices must be undisciplined and released on the mainstream. By the way, can you recommend
a few pieces on feminist theory to read before the conference?*

Warm regards,

JUSOFS

Scene 1

*The conference participants, having breakfasted on decaffeinated
coffee, cholesterol-inhibiting oat bran muffins, and fiber-filled
fruit, are settling down to pursue their dialogue. The setting is a
large university where a well-known group of scholars in international relations have congratulated themselves on being open-
minded enough to sponsor this dialogue, albeit few among them
are in the audience. Some graduate students in attendance quietly
take their seats, close enough to the participants to hear but far
enough away to denote their inferior status.*

SAR: We left off last time with JUSOFS commenting in three alter-
nating voices—postmodernist, new left, and a critical perspective—on my delusions about the autonomy of science from realism, especially in the science-driven realist United States,
and, by implication, my delusion about keeping fairly free from
realist prejudices in my own scientific work.

JUSOFS: Yes, but I believe you were maneuvering around the substance of my criticisms by accusing me of harboring contradictory voices. What makes you think there is *a* view somewhere *out there* or *a* method for finding such *a* view that erases or should erase inconsistency, contradiction ...

SAR: Oh please, let's not slog around in social science methods 101. Surely you know that scientific theories do not erase all doubt and inconsistency. Rather, they bring doubts to light by providing reasonable starting points, agreed-upon standpoints for hypothesis formation and testing.

JUSOFS: Yes, but the methods both expose the inconsistencies in the theory and tame them to fit the agreed-upon standpoint. Look at the theory of general nuclear deterrence. It starts historically with the idea that nuclear weapons are different from conventional weapons—"by convention—by an understanding, a tradition, a consensus, a shared willingness to see them as different."[8] The strategic thinker then plots ways to impose usable order on that disordering difference, bearing in mind that, unlike conventional weapons, nukes can simultaneously devastate an enemy—win the war—and provoke a last-gasp counterattack that also "wins" the war. The presumed constancy of hostile intent between the superpowers is a starting point for a theory of peace, backed up by hardware, in which we stabilize the nuclear difference by embodying a threat to hurt the enemy badly if he steps over a particular line. Enter the hypothesis testers who seek to quantify "hurt" and ascertain how much hurt is tolerable and credibly returnable if "they" hurt "us" first. This entry of science gets the game theorists excited, and they rush to calculate how many options two or more deterrence-gaming adversaries have in a variety of single or iterated moves. De-terr-ence becomes the reign of terror created to rein in the nuclear terror, and those who try to interrogate or de-tour it are called names, accused of questionable political loyalties, simply ignored, and so on.

SAR: I think I need more coffee for this. Lots of strong coffee.

JUSOFS (*without missing a beat*): The idea that accumulated anomalies or inconsistencies and other considerations can cause an eventual paradigm shift sounds naive in this context. If general deterrence theory is breaking down now—and, of course, "there has emerged in the global community a recognition that nuclear weapons are unusable across much of the range of traditional military and political interests"[9]—how much does the breakdown have to do with actions of ordinary East European people in ending the Cold War, vis-à-vis the revelations of experts that nuclear weapons can no longer reinforce Cold War hegemonies anyway? Are we following a people's agenda, a scientific agenda, or both? Even as we study change in the international system, will we deter inconsistent findings and questions, ignore other considerations, and subvert alternative knowledges in order to maintain the falsehood that science is not only objective on national or other considerations but is the only "true" view in town?

WESTFEM: Bravo JUSOFS! A tour de force, really. But what do you mean by "other considerations," and whom do you have in mind when you say "ordinary East European people"? Who are "the people" in Eastern Europe?

JUSOFS: Other considerations? Well, think of the class biases encapsulated in our theories of deterrence. Is deterrence not a theory designed to protect the knowledge and power of weapons producers and wielders? Also, SAR and I spoke last time about the luxury of being an academic in the U.S.; I still maintain that the good academic life blinded senior scholars to urgent "considerations" in the world, such as poverty.

WESTFEM: I see. But aren't you missing something?

JUSOFS: I know, I know. You're getting at the fact that women are often silenced components of "the people" and that men's voices are often very loud but unacknowledged as sources of gendered knowledge.

WESTFEM: Sounds like you've heard this gender reminder before, and yet you still fail to mention it as a "consideration" unless prompted to do so.

JUSOFS: I protest! Some of my colleagues now point to the sovereign voice of Man in IR theory and consider the ways in which

concepts dear to this field were masculinized by the early political theorists.[10] For myself, I think that playing around with nuclear weapons can be a gendered activity that draws on what
we usually think of as masculine constructions of power and
defense (rather than an activity in which only males figure, for
there are females involved in smaller numbers).

WESTFEM: The point is that all types of IR theorists can sometimes
see the masculine bias in supposedly objective theory. But
rarely can they see or recuperate the activities of people called
women within those theories.

JUSOFS: You know some of the reasons for that: Statecraft is
mancraft,[11] and theorycraft is sorely bereft of feminist standpoint—that is, of the insights feminists have achieved by drawing on the subordinated voices of women in most societies.[12]
I've just read, for instance, that women are prone to a morality
of care, which suggests that the "justice" of deterrence would
always have been secondary to women relative to concerns
with maintaining human connectedness.[13] Ah, but we must
also raise the question of whether "women" or "men" even exist except as categories to justify an unequal distribution of material power.

WESTFEM: Hold on. You're not wrong in what you say, but you are
spouting some undigested feminism. If women contribute to
strategic calculations, are they men in drag? Do all men engage
in statecraft? Are all women pacifists and smiley-faced peace
signers? Or are those the rules under the caricatures of gender?
Which of many feminist standpoints would correct these gender biases? Is all science bad and all critique space-expanding
and democratic? Is positing the unreality of gender categories
merely a new strategy for erasing women before we can find
out what people walking around in women's bodies think
about things and how we …

JUSOFS: Wait a minute, I'm simply …

SAR: Maybe we're getting a little off the track here?

TSITSI: I certainly hope so. What JUSOFS is saying implies that the
average Zimbabwean man is a realist itching to get his fingers

on a weapons control panel because he is implicated in masculine IR statecraft. It's only the Big Men who take their pleasures this way. The men in our society have their privileges and are often violent with us. And yes, a good many of them used women during the independence war. But there are differences between superpower and underpower men. In Zimbabwe, when men fight a war, they fight and then stop. They don't stockpile weapons as a way of preventing the next one. And what about the notion that real women always eschew violence? That's precisely what our government now wants people to believe about Zimbabwean women—that we're really traditionalists in the sense of cooking *sadza,* having babies, and getting bossed by men. "Introducing masculinity into a discussion of international politics, and thereby making men visible as men, should prompt us to explore differences in the politics of masculinity between countries."[14] And to say that women and men may not exist except as categories of inequality is really one of the silliest things I've heard in a long time. Leave it to postmodernists like JUSOFS to think of this one!

WESTFEM: From where I sit, TSITSI, I can't help but see things a bit differently. In Zimbabwe, women's participation in the armed struggle for independence transgressed the usual boundaries of gender and, in effect, trampled on men's self-claimed property rights to war.[15] When the shooting ended, the disciplining agencies of the Zimbabwean state cracked down on women's transgressing war labor and reasserted another gendered property right, that of pronouncing women as mothers and family members, first and foremost. This erasure of women from "our" particular history of competence in defeating enemies in local shooting wars has a counterpart in the erasure of "women" as agents of national politics and the international politics of states.

TSITSI: Hmm.

WESTFEM: Also, I can't take a lot of solace in the idea that your men are not stockpiling weapons, by which I assume you mean that they haven't tried militarily to deter the former Rhodesians from holding on to land and perks in the new Zimbabwe. Your men are prevented from stockpiling conventional or nuclear weapons by shortages in foreign exchange in the world system of capitalism. Moreover, the superpowers don't allow most underpower men to have nukes. Nonetheless, I've watched many men in Zimbabwe stockpile beer, robbing their children of school fees in the process. And I've seen them try to deter women from taking active roles in the state and in the workplace. There may be peace in Zimbabwe, but it is a patriarchal peace.[16] Indeed, are not average Zimbabwean men carriers of the privilege accorded your own Big Men who sit at the helm of statecraft? And is it not possible that "women's capacity to challenge the men in their families, their communities or their political movements will be a key to remaking the world?"[17]

TSITSI: Ah, I see these points. But many of my sisters say that we women, "because of the negative and destructive effects of historical processes and racism on Africa and its people, [have developed] values stressing human totality, parallel autonomy, cooperation, self-reliance, adaptation, survival, and liberation,"[18] that we value male-female complementarity. I don't know what I think about women saying this, since our "men say they want to preserve their culture from western influence … when they feel threatened by women."[19]

WESTFEM: A-men!

TSITSI: Some African feminists, though, would say that men and the state go together because there are parallel spheres of gender autonomy in our societies—men run the state and women run the household.

WESTFEM: Yet you talk about Zimbabwean women guerrillas as people who were neither in nor out of the state, in nor out of the household when they became woman combatants. There may be a false dichotomy between statecraft-mancraft and homecraft-womencraft as parallel spheres. A smudging of the line seems more expressive of the experiences of "women combatants" and maybe even of some "homecrafters" in Zimbabwe.

JUSOFS: Of course, that's part of the postmodernist search for political spaces in-between the usual oppositions.

SAR (*sighing*): This is all very interesting, but how does it relate to international relations?

TSITSI (*under her breath to WESTFEM*): Here we go. The super-power representatives are now going to pronounce international relations for us.

WESTFEM: SAR, there is implied hegemony in your question. I thought you were trying to convince JUSOFS last time that you didn't follow fashion in the days of realist hegemony, that you broke with the nonscientific discourse of the day in order to follow your scientific inclinations? How can you now say that "our" unconventional discussion is irrelevant to IR?

SAR: I was unconventional within the parameters of agreement on what constituted international relations as a subject matter separate from other subjects like literary theory or women's studies. The IR focus is more or less on states as actors, international structures of production and exchange, international regime formation, foreign policy decisionmaking, and so on. Now there are people exploring codeterminations of international structures and processes. Maybe that's where this discussion fits. I'm somewhat in that camp these days.[20]

WESTFEM: And where are the "women"? Are we "outside" all those definitional categories of IR by virtue of being placed "inside" the private households situated "inside" domestic society? If so, that puts us at least two layers from official agency in IR. We do not exist there.

SAR: Oh, Lord. I need more coffee.

JUSOFS: I'll go with you.

WESTFEM: Not so fast. Maria Mies and Cynthia Enloe have pointed out that a lot of women-bodied beings are in the thick of international political economy. Consumers buy TVs produced by women working for multinational companies in Asia. Women support the high classifiers of secrets when we are diplomats' wives or secretaries. Our vacations to third world countries bring needed foreign exchange, and our laundry adds to the work of underpaid chambermaids. A few of us, like Pocahontas and Chiquita Banana, become informal emissaries for our states.[21] Amidst all this activity, it happens that we are not the "we" or the "they" who are the "decisionmakers" in IR. In IR, "what we look for has an effect on what we find,"[22] and "we" commonly don't look for "women."

TSITSI: WESTFEM is saying, and I happen to agree with her, that only when women bear arms or serve as heads of state do we seem to simultaneously challenge both the gender boundary that forces us into peaceful domesticity and the IR boundary that protects us within confining nations from the dangers of international relations. But when we do transgress such boundaries, women combatants are soon back in the land of angel food cakes and *sadza* and the spaces in-between, for our new "roles" in society are blocked—sometimes by a woman head of state who rewards patriarchs for tolerating her violation of the "rules" that stipulate who may rightfully lead a nation.

WESTFEM: Frankly, I wonder about an in-between venue to national-international relations that features women combatants. The good soldier may bear a strong resemblance to the good mother—both of them, for instance, are immersed in concerns with bodily harm, and both are "racked by guilt at not having done it right or at having done wrong as they did what they thought was right."[23] But this similarity may simply mean that there are grave problems both with soldiering and mothering. Maybe we can say the same for mothering and leading *a* nation.

SAR: If women are already in IR—and I'm more than willing to concede that they and others have "a perceived right to undertake action in global affairs"[24]—is there a feminist model of the field that does away with these "grave problems" and with the biases of mainstream theory and women-eclipsing practice?

TSITSI: You will want to ask me as well as her. Salman Rushdie may partly justify *Satanic Verses* by saying that we third worlders and you first worlders are all "leaking into each other."[25] That's a good homogenizing image. But many of us ex-

perience and want to preserve our differences even while recognizing those leaks, and those differences may well extend to
our respective interpretations of international relations. When
you and even WESTFEM speak of a "state," a woman in Zimbabwe might think of the authority of a "household." We are the
ones who can really turn your world topsy, unless, that is, you
label our concerns "incommensurable" with yours.

WESTFEM: You illustrated the point nicely: There is no one feminist model of IR. Instead, variously situated feminists, like
TSITSI-I, point out how some presences within IR are formed,
sidetracked, and forced outside by the keepers of theories and
practices of IR. Feminists also discuss how the situation would
look if we outsiders were welcomed back in—how some states
would look, how nations would be understood, how decisions
would be made. Important too is that we ask whether states,
nations, and conventional leaders would even be centerpiece
concepts any longer in a field of theory informed by feminist
thinking. In these tasks we are doing feminist IR even though IR
"experts" say we are only talking about doing feminist IR. One
analyst, in fact, challenged us "to contrast a feminist construction of international security with a neo-realist one."[26] For him
there's *a* way of doing IR and we're just not doing it yet.

TSITSI: I surely hope, though, that feminists will consider factors
other than gender when evaluating biases in IR theory and
when considering what can be done to bring in other ways of
theorizing. It is important to note real national, cultural, racial,
and class differences as well as the possibility that differing
gender experiences may not produce uniform identities for
women and men around the world. Within an appreciation of
differences, we can then find areas of feminist solidarity.

SAR: Now we're back on the track of national considerations—at
last.

TSITSI: Let me add, though, that it's necessary to avoid the "strait-
jacketing effect of [all] sovereign categories."[27] I mean, we don't
want to assume that race, class, or "national considerations"
are so real that "other considerations," such as gender, pale
alongside them. That's what happened in the past: The Marx-

ists said that class is all-important; people of color pointed at race; and some historians told us about the centrality of national considerations to the outcomes of history. In this litany of important factors, it happened time and again that gender was forgotten. Let's make sure we aren't so ecumenical in our approach that we end up deemphasizing gender relative to other sources of perspective.

SAR: Sounds to me as though feminists want to implicate gender in everything. There is considerable abstract structure in the international system. If you're a realist you see sovereign states pursuing national interests within a distinct distribution of material power—a certain balance of power. If you're a neoliberal institutionalist, you see egoistic states building patterns of cooperation in order to avoid the consequences of unregulated acts. Even if we assume that the international system is in flux and transition, we can appreciate the presence and functioning of stable structures—the chaos that hints at coherence.[28] We have bedrocks to the field that the feminists and postmodernists want either to deny—that seems to be the postmodernist game—or replace with "other considerations" like gender.

JUSOFS: SAR, there has never really been that bedrock of IR, that Rosetta stone of international relations we can use to unlock the door of some essential Truth. There has simply been a series of assertions about the fundamentals of the field, and with the constant assertions has come the power to narrate them into a shadowy existence. In other words, the characteristics of the international system are not given. They're created by IR discourse. Ask people who aren't scientists what the international system looks like, or even whether they think it exists, and they might not see what you see. Is that because they are untrained in our field, or because the power to narrate is conspicuously at work to distance the "true" story of international relations from the stories of dissidents?

SAR: Truth or Dissidence?

JUSOFS: It's more like Truth *and* Dissidence. Most debates in the field—say, between traditionalists and scientists, on the one hand, and realists and neoliberal institutionalists, on the other—have been akin to controversies within one small church. One could argue that parsimony and elegance have operated to keep dissidents out of most images of the world, and that means there are still many voices in a limbo exile—*of* IR but not officially *in* it.[29]

WESTFEM: Moreover, you misunderstand feminism if you think that we want to make gender a new bedrock of IR. We're revealing a chorus of masculine voices that has heretofore been deemed normal in the field. Some feminist standpointers, I guess, want to replace the music sung by the chorus as well as its gender composition, but arguably they seek to do this in order to get all of us away from the tyranny of monotonal voice in IR.

SAR: I don't know. I think there have been cycles of theory,[30] each with a slightly different notion of the essentials of IR. Now, historical circumstances lend themselves to the inclusion of more essentials than ever before, and a cooperative reconceptualization of the field makes sense. That's why I invited you here today.

TSITSI: Yes, thank you. But let me say that ever since the independence negotiations on Zimbabwe, which took place between representatives of Great Britain, Rhodesia, and the guerrilla fighting forces, I've been suspicious of "cooperative reconceptualizations." When people have different power statuses, the cooperations tend to be stacked against the historically weaker sides. Zimbabwe has turned out well, compared to other countries in Africa that went through armed struggles for independence. But much of the guerrilla agenda of that struggle was compromised and bargained away at that negotiating table because Great Britain's voice and vote seemed to count for more than anyone else's—the voices of Zimbabwean women had already been subsumed in the "national" guerrilla agenda. So when we talk about a "cooperative reconceptualization of international relations," I can't help but ask whose expectations will be in the lead? Whose essentials will swallow up the agenda of "ordinary people"?

SAR: You certainly raise some important points. But international relations is in flux, in part, because ordinary dissident voices are shaking things up. That is the lesson of East Germany.

TSITSI: Still, I worry. Will "our" field build theory for a new era that simply puts together a novel form of masculine voice? Or is it possible for the field to enter an as yet undefined period of posthegemony beyond the truth and dissidence cycle of usual theory?[31]

WESTFEM: This particular issue brings to mind a time, not so long ago, when members of the World Order Models Project [WOMP][32] suggested a range of alternative world futures, each based on a particular national or regional standpoint. The IR experts generally smirked at the project. The irony there, besides the fact that some of the aspects of those alternative visions did indeed come true after 1989, is that the WOMP models were crafted, to a one, by men—who arguably shared some similar standpoints on power, cooperation, and so forth with the expert IR men judging them. Still, the field laughed. Notwithstanding the argument that the time for blueprints is over, why would laughter not ring out were feminist outsiders to craft alternatives? There's an old trap out there and it's called: Give us an alternative and "we'll" consider its merits for you.

SAR: Penalty! At the time, it seemed that those WOMP futures simply weren't in the cards because they relied on good faith changes by current power holders. Also, they weren't verifiable and persuasive to science—and to realpolitik—minded colleagues. WOMP seemed to be an exercise in abstract modeling beyond the pale or at the fringes of empirical realities.

TSITSI: Ah, but the people of East Berlin forced "good faith changes" onto current power holders. And they did it, by and large, by strolling past the Wall pushing baby carriages and by gathering in the streets of Dresden. Tell me, are people-led changes in Eastern Europe and South Africa persuasive, or are they at the fringe of *an* empirical reality that doesn't fit *the* models offered by science- and realpolitik-minded colleagues?

SAR: They're quite persuasive, and it bothers me that some theorists—and many U.S. decisionmakers—claim that hardline

U.S. policy or the example of western democracy caused those changes. In point of fact, many of us did not predict the timing of recent upheavals in the turbulent system. Now I detect a longing in some quarters for the certainty of the old game of Cold War Truth (and Silenced Dissidents).

JUSOFS: I'm not surprised. There are many IR types who would benefit from reinstating such a reality.

SAR: But we foil reactionary sentiment like that best when we develop sound theory. Isn't that what all of us want, irrespective of our particular national or gender or philosophical circumstances?

TSITSI: But SAR, for many feminists, pieces of the Berlin Wall still stand—the turbulent system isn't turbulent enough—because "our" analyses are not entering the discussions of global change carried on under the banner of a more open world.[33] Power may now be more dispersed in the world, but when does turbulence become a "revolution"? I think something's still missing when seemingly profound changes, as we see in South Africa and Eastern Europe, circulate only male-bodied persons through the state—even if those bodies are inhabited by somewhat unmasculine personalities, like the new hero, Vaclav Havel. Under this type of change, the bodies of women and other invisibles melt away into a silent support role for the new leaders. Then, indeed, for whom is "sound theory" and action progressive?

WESTFEM: That question may be difficult to answer given that the modern notion of *a* revolution seems to miss the simultaneity of revolutionary actions visible across the turbulent world today.[34] I'm troubled by the question of who should draft the parameters of inclusivity. I watched the Federal Republic of Germany "codetermining" the future of Germany with the former German Democratic Republic and sensed that a more extended period of pluralist debate would have been preferable to the rushed convergence. Yet who am I to say? It's not my context. "The people" in the GDR were shouting for unity, unity, unity even as feminist groups in the GDR struggled to formulate a new catalog of demands.[35] Now, do these former GDR "women" exist?

TSITSI: It's a most vexing issue, this point of democratic input, and one all of us need to ponder in nonabstract ways. Otherwise where are we? Whose theory is "our" theory?

JUSOFS: In case no one has noticed, postmodernists have already identified many of the theoretical problems we are raising here.

TSITSI: You have, and I applaud your efforts. But I would like to take this chance to say that postmodernists spend altogether too much time reevaluating texts produced by the Big Men of western philosophy and noting how many of their ideas have been misunderstood and erroneously appropriated to support contemporary mainstream IR thinking. Given all your efforts to reinterpret Hobbes, Machiavelli, and the other white boys, isn't it time we looked at the ancient, modern, and contemporary voices of nonBig, nonWhite, nonMen? Not to do so suggests that "many male postmodernists [are] unaware of the deeply gendered nature of their own recounting and interpretations of 'the' western story and the strategies they oppose to its 'master narratives.' 'Man' retains his privileged place as the sole author and principal character in their stories."[36]

WESTFEM: Fortunately, the feminists have already learned from our own period of myopia. In the 1970s, western feminists endeavored to set up ideal-typical models of "woman"—as lesbian, mother, peace-lover, worker, and so on—that would supposedly apply to women in places like Zimbabwe *and* to rich ladies on Park Avenue in New York. We took a lot of criticism for that—many calls of imperialism revisited—and we learned from it.[37]

TSITSI: That's right. No one was asking us then how "our" lives played out and why "our" women weren't embodied in those models. At the same time, if postmodernists now respond to our objections by politely ignoring us because they are aware of problems in representation, then if they wait for us to represent ourselves, or if they erase us by saying that gender doesn't really exist, so let's talk about something else, we will have problems being heard. Those with power just don't seem anxious to allow the represented to represent ourselves. At least that's how the "power structure" of IR, as subject matter and as subject actors, looks to me—and male postmodernists are part of that picture. It is the same in "modern" Zimbabwe—only a handful of women are in parliament with ministry portfolios, and sometimes they are brought in only if they cheerlead for the status quo—or for the transformations the men are leading.

SAR: But isn't postmodernism the latest craze in feminism? Shouldn't you and JUSOFS be more in agreement?

WESTFEM: Your question suggests that " 'postmodernism' exists as an emergent ideology demanding partisan allegiance … [and] doctrinaire adherents."[38] I think you're projecting the creed of science onto us. We don't want to recreate boundaries of identity that make it possible for some people to be identified with certain realms of knowledge and power (international-men) while others are located outside (families-women). That is why some of us prefer to speak of a postmodern turn in feminism— rather than feminist postmodernism per se, which merely has us cheerleading for some male-invented postmodernism. The postmodern turn enables feminists—the skeptics about truth, identity, and theory developed to explain modern, women-eclipsing life—to evaluate the social constitution of gender categories rather than seize on some true theory or practice (the designation of "women" and "men," for example) as a guide to correct behavior.[39] Through deconstructing the great and small texts of IR to see who is missing or falsely represented, through genealogical studies of the power laden in the enunciation of gender assignments, and through a careful inclusion of ourselves as authorities into the research at hand, we postmodern feminists of the west hope to assess "the very criteria by which claims to knowledge are legitimized."[40]

TSITSI: I'm gratified to hear you say "of the west," because I think that feminists in my part of the world are more feminist stand-point–oriented; that is, more certain that women really exist as subordinated members of the species—to men, to westerners, to capitalism—you name it. This business of women not existing is really over the top and politically dangerous. Look, I'm here in front of you—a woman—and as a woman I am adding my voice to this dialogue. Would I be here otherwise?

WESTFEM: Excellent points. I don't think it's silly, however, to ponder the possibility that "men" and "women" are not natural essences but rather manmade categories of identity, power, and knowledge. People designated as "women," are kept in our places by common sense and practice and by scientifically "validated" truths about how men and women really are as naturalized beings (you know, women are bad at math). We join a host of other outsiders—for example, third worlders and working-class male laborers—who seemingly have nothing to add to the august field of international relations unless we speak the accepted tongue and append ourselves to the approved community of wisdom. In this I agree with the general tenor of postmodernism.

JUSOFS: Yes, of course.

WESTFEM: I also agree with postmodernists that subjugated sites of knowledge and power resist the discipline imposed on them by the purveyors of truth. Some "women," for instance, eschew the notion that strong allies must protect weaker partners by sharing "our" nuclear weapons with them. Instead, they set up women's peace encampments (such as Greenham Common) with nonhierarchical, nonlinear, and nonreciprocal methods for arriving at strategies, which the campers think of as prefiguratively anticipating "a simple, peaceful, postnuclear society."[41] The strategy of the camps emerges through deep conversations, with everyone listening and being partly transformed by the conversation. That is a far cry from the type of dialogue we are having here, which features (mostly) separate individuals with separate points of view trying to win by convincing others to change loyalties and identities.[42]

TSITSI: Wait a minute. I'm confused here. I thought you were defending the need to deconstruct received categories such as men/women. Now I hear you talking about peace camps that people, whom you uncritically accept as women, established to challenge the combat posture of the strategic community.

WESTFEM: I'm indeed sliding back and forth, forward and backward around the concept "women." I assume, on the one hand, that the term "women" masks a plethora of identities that exist as gaps in the representations of us that are prevalent in official knowledge; in that sense "women" is a created identity. On the other hand, I have some sympathy with the feminist standpoint position that holds that we must work with the category "women" and identify the standpoints that people called "women" have on a host of topics; we cannot evacuate the site of "women" without silencing all the people who currently identify with that label, thereby undercutting our power.

TSITSI (*folding her arms across her chest*): Then we agree a bit.

WESTFEM: Yes, especially when you consider the logistical problems that standpoint and postmodern feminists share: how to ensure "that everyone has a chance to speak … that each voice counts equally; how to assess whether equality or participation is necessary in all cases or in which cases; how to effect a transition from the present in which many voices cannot speak, are necessarily excluded, or are not heard to a more pluralist one; how to instill and guarantee a preference for speaking over the use of force; and how to compensate for the political consequences of an unequal distribution and control of resources."[43]

TSITSI: In other words, because you're a feminist—an analyst who recognizes that people called women have been left out of many a democratizing scheme—you can appreciate many points in postmodernism, particularly its emphasis on dissident voices, and also remain somewhat skeptical on other points of process and methodology.

WESTFEM: Right.

JUSOFS: But how can you even temporarily preserve "women" as an identity and not also preserve other identities and categories, such as "men"? Wouldn't this approach lead us back to the status quo?

WESTFEM: Good question. I don't want to reinforce "a suspicion that deconstructive politics may be most appealing to those who are accustomed to and confident of having their voices heard in almost any conversation and therefore feel no particular need to be worried about such 'details.' "[44]

SAR: Whew!

WESTFEM: So let me say all of this yet another way. It strikes me that "women" is an invention. But "we" must not be defined out of existence before the knowledges of people who have been in "our" subject position come to the fore. To kill women off too early is possibly to hand power to those who have been privileged in the past and who still can be heard before we are heard. This is not to say that all identities must be or even can be preserved. Postmodernist men bring new masculine voices to IR only to find themselves treated like women by the Old Boys of the field. There's already much slippage at the gender gates, and "women" can add to ongoing decentering tendencies by not rushing to plunge the dagger into "us" until "we" have made more "progress" in being heard as women.

TSITSI: The field of IR is certainly righteous about its boundaries, and that speaks volumes about the challenges ahead.

SAR: I like your last point.

WESTFEM: I think a willingness to situate oneself with "IR," "postmodernism," "feminism," or "women" and yet be critical of these identities is indeed preferable to clinging to the position that the problematiques are incommensurable, which, by the way, is how I read SAR's and JUSOFS' first dialogue of the deaf. This is a lesson we can draw from the global women's movement. Prior to the more empathizing United Nations Conference on Women, held in Nairobi in 1985, western and African women tended to criticize each other, as if we were the ones holding ourselves back. In 1985, we women stopped yelling at each other quite so much and started focusing on our points of tangency in difference.

TSITSI: Whenever there are stark standoffs, I'm reminded of the Zimbabwean government's defensive clinging to a wartime Marxist-Leninist True Story through the 1980s, despite the strong capitalist policies it pursued and all the ideological struggles that were calling Marxism-Leninism into question.[45] By contrast, look at the quantities of humble pie being consumed in the erstwhile Soviet Union. Look at how Gorbachev approached the United States, hat in hand, for foreign aid. Such Big Men put themselves into a governance problematique that their own theories and processes had a hand in creating, but that they could have tried to disavow as ruinous dissidence or bourgeois revisionism.

WESTFEM: There's a certain power in humility. Maybe Gorbachev and his cronies have paved a new road for IR, just as the more arrogant and violent behaviors of the superpowers helped carve a Cold War path at a certain moment in history. The next generation of graduate students may well study the diplomacy of humility along with the diplomacy of force and threat. The incommensurables will become commensurable, not because the latter tames the former, one hopes, but because relational autonomy—the simultaneous attachment of the separate problematiques—will be respected.

(*There is a stir among the outsiders within the dialogue as "graduate student" becomes a recognized subject category. But still these subalterns do not speak.*)[46]

WESTFEM: Yes, imagine a time when we move back and forth among our multiple identities as scientists, postmodernists, and feminists, calling first on one approach and then on another and maybe on several simultaneously as respected ways of knowing across a range of topics.[47] Imagine moving back and forth across the territories of "men" and "women."

SAR: For many, humility will surely take all the fun out of academic IR.

JUSOFS (*laughing*): Indeed!

SAR: In fact, can't all those identities be accommodated within empirical analysis, that is to say, within science? Can't we separate the effects of gender bias on IR the way I think we can separate science from the national agendas of realism?

(*Silence.*)

SAR: Er, no doubt we can make that accommodation.

(*Silence.*)

JUSOFS: Yes, but can you discipline IR's audience to accept that expertise as EXPERTISE?

TSITSI-WESTFEM: It depends on how you define "our IR," don't you think? Good evening, gentle men.

Scene 2

TSITSI-WESTFEM is experiencing that twilight consciousness that comes when the body does not know where it is and the attached mind follows its whims.

TSITSI: We're almost home. Just two hours before we land in Harare.

WESTFEM: Yes. Home. Zimbabwe. Africa. Home?

TSITSI: Yes, you know you always feel especially good when you're in Harare. You always say things go well for you here. You slip into a felicitous identity and leave the other tired identities at home. So, we're almost "home."

WESTFEM: Hmm. They say (you know all those "theys"—they include "us") that this thing called postmodernism is dangerously nihilistic. Yet surely this is one of life's intriguing postmodern moments: in-between homes and identities like East Berliners walking across to West Berlin in 1989, like Communists instituting more free-market conditions.

(*Silence.*)

WESTFEM: I wonder whether U.S. fighter pilots experienced identity slippage like this as they headed north from Saudi Arabia in 1991 with their deadly cargoes? Every message at hand screamed at them: You are not-Iraqi. And yet what is postcombat syndrome if not wartime identities and memories that refuse subjugation and silence in peacetime?

TSITSI: What about nationalism? What about all those parades in the United States when the victorious troops returned? I didn't notice any ambiguous identities in that display. I noticed only the standpointed view of people who had won a war and now had the right to narrate history in their own terms. Interestingly, those "people" included a black commander and a few women—indeed, enough women that the U.S. government became intrigued with the notion that women could be combatants. What has happened to the outsiders of IR? Have we been pulled inside or are we now witnessing the era of diversity?

WESTFEM: I don't see militaries as sites of tolerance for diversity, so I guess we're seeing the broadening of subject identities for women and other heretofore quieted voices only as long as they are willing to speak the military tongue. But, of course, you never know what the infusion of different knowledge into the military ultimately does to it. After all, our identities do shift a bit, and "soldier" may come to be profoundly reinterpreted by "women" soldiers, although I must admit to skepticism on that point.[48] As for the certainties displayed in the parades, well …

(*Silence.*)

TSITSI: Ah, wouldn't it be fascinating to study this! We could do a comparative research project on Zimbabwean and U.S. nationalist fervor following "our" latest respective victories—us over the Rhodesians in 1980 and the U.S. over the Iraqis in 1991.

(*Silence.*)

WESTFEM: Yes. We would need to understand the construction of identity through these wars by evaluating the songs, slogans, media portrayals, and stories that inscribed nationalist identity on so many bodies. And we'd have to talk to "noncombatants" to evaluate that line between combatant and noncombatant. Along the way we'd keep an eye out for the slogans not chosen, the subtexts and surplus meanings in the stories that may defy the soldiering behaviors, the resistances to discipline as well as the complicities hidden in the words, grammars, and symbols of nationalism.

(*Silence.*)

TSITSI: Yes, I like this. It's right up my alleys.

WESTFEM: Alley.

TSITSI: No, no. There are many to explore, eh? And I think I see the value in that postmodern turn to the notion that life experiences form texts open to various readings and interpretations. It makes sense to me that seemingly strong moments of nationalism are more ambiguous and less unified than meets the eye and that one can see this in simple things: Is not a "ticker tape" the guts of finance capital displaying its continuously unraveling, but precarious and paper-like victories? Isn't a victory "parade" in some senses a ra(i)d(e) on or a sign of a successful (s)par with mortality?

WESTFEM: You sound like me now. Except for one thing. Where are the feminist angles in your-our research? That postmodern turn in IR is in "our" employ when we're feminists. We craft it to be sensitive to us, something it doesn't seem especially inclined to be on its own.

TSITSI: The feminist angles are everywhere, if we will see them, if we will think about the topic at hand as a terrain of gender scriptings and practices and resist all tiresome suggestions that what we are researching is the woman's angle on recent wars. You know my dear, "women" may not exist.

WESTFEM: Who's going home? Sounds to me like you're increasingly at home in a way of thinking that is the product of western uncertainties about theory and truth in a discombobulated late twentieth century.

TSITSI: Never fear, I insist on my different identity hyphenations. You are coming home, but you have too many identities at odds with "Zimbabwean" to be coming home for good. I have too many identities resisting "westernizations" to be completely at home with this so-called postmodern turn. Wouldn't it be nice if most international relations theorists could get that point—that where you sit depends on where you stand in a shifting array of identities that, nonetheless for us, at least, never strays too far from something we can call "feminist?"

(*Silence.*)

WESTFEM: You know, it's funny—all the handwringing going on in

IR, all the accusations that this theory and that regional specialist did not predict the momentous changes of 1989 and beyond in Eastern Europe, South Africa, and even in the Middle East. Silly, really. Prediction can tame events. What we have seen is a series of peoples' refusals of tamings such as this. That "our" theories are in a shambles and "our" university courses in disarray gives me hope that "our" minds are similarly open to the (only seemingly) incommensurabilities of the era. But I doubt we are humbled.

TSITSI: From where I sit, we will only be humbled when we stop stockpiling the scripts of Big Men, hosing them down, and returning them to positions of prominence in an era when the activities of ordinary people in the streets of the world are re-scripting those scripts.

WESTFEM: Are they? Or are they toppling the figureheads and leaving the pylons standing?

TSITSI: "We are different in different 'worlds' and ourselves in them."[49] There's space for maneuver.

Long silence. Lightning below. Zaire slips into Zambia. The engines hum and the "stewardesses" prepare for breakfast. All "our" work continues at a quarter to 747.

ACT III

Hegemonic Power, Hegemonic Discipline? The Superpower Status of the American Study of International Relations

Steve Smith

Scene 1

Two men are standing in line outside a bathroom in a modern British university residence hall. The older one, SUKA (Senior U.K. Academic), smiles benignly at an obviously impatient IRTS (International Relations Theory Scholar).

SUKA: You mustn't be so impatient at having to queue up for the bathroom. It's one of the delights of coming to the BISA [British International Studies Association] conference each December. Americans would doubtless call it quaint.

IRTS: Quaint it may be; delightful it is not. I really get annoyed with the facilities we have to put up with each year. Americans would never put up with this type of thing. They have their conferences in big, plush hotels, where you actually have several bars and specially designed meeting rooms. Nothing like our annual conferences, where we have to stay in student study-bedrooms with toilets several minutes' walk down unheated corridors, eat in the one refectory, with menus that make airplane food look like gastronomic delights, and hold our meetings in university seminar rooms that have broken chairs and drafty windows.

SUKA: Yes, but don't forget the different costs involved. BISA this time cost us, what, £72 [$115] for registration, two nights' accommodation, and three meals a day. At the U.S. ISA [International Studies Association] conference you pay $40 just to register and then something like $100 a day for the room, which, remember, doesn't include any meals. That means that the conference probably costs a U.S. academic around $650 without travel costs.

IRTS: Agreed, but they get paid a lot more. I mean, what is the top of the career grade in Britain, about £22,000 [$35,000] a year?

SUKA: £22,400, in fact, with the top professors earning no more than around £33,000 [$52,500] a year.

IRTS: Yes, but we all know that in the U.K. there's usually only one professor in any one department. And, more important, U.S. academics get their conference expenses paid by their universities. At my place we have an allowance of only £150 [$240] a year for all our research and conference activity. We even have to buy our own word processors! Last year, the library book budget ran out three months into the financial year, so we couldn't buy any books for the next nine months. Anyway, that isn't what bothers me. I think that U.S. conferences are vastly superior to our own. Look at this one: We have about 180 members attending, and that's our biggest turnout ever. We have about four panels at any one time, with three papers per panel. That means a maximum of seventy-two papers in the entire conference. At the ISA, there are about twenty panels at any time, with fourteen sessions and an average of three papers a panel. That equals about a thousand papers! We are such a small operation, no wonder we can't compete with the U.S. when it comes to the development of the subject.

SUKA: Hang on a minute. Don't confuse quantity with quality. Have you been to ISA? Sometimes there are more people on the panel than in the audience—the audience introduces itself to the panel. Anyway, sure, maybe 1,500 attend the conference, but at any time one-third are at the book exhibit or in the bar, one-third are sightseeing, and the third who hear the papers end up wishing they hadn't. At the last ISA panel I went to, for example, the three presenters took twenty minutes each, followed by two discussants who took fifteen minutes each, which left fifteen minutes for so-called discussion, most of which was taken up with what an American friend of mine calls "station-identification."

IRTS: But at least a lot happens at their conferences.

SUKA: Don't be too impressed by the size of their conferences. Were you at the 1989 joint ISA/BISA conference? The original idea was for each panel to feature half Brits and half ISA. That looked fine in South Carolina, but when we worked out the implications, we realized that every BISA member attending would have to give 3.3 papers, chair .84 of a panel, and act as discussant on 1.68 occasions. It really is a mistake to be so impressed by the size of U.S. conferences.

IRTS: Perhaps we should ...

SUKA: I'll tell you what gave me the biggest laugh at the ISA/BISA conference: the size of badges. We Brits had our modest handwritten cards, with our names so small that you had to squint to see them. The Americans had massive printed postcard-sized things, proudly proclaiming their institutional affiliation in letters that could be read from ten feet. They even had some kind of plastic covering, but maybe that was just in case the English weather let us down.

IRTS: Ah, but you know quantity has a quality all its own. The U.S. academic community has dominated the subject of international relations since the Second World War, and there really is no way that we in the rest of the world can do anything other than respond to their initiatives. Which reminds me, I've been invited to talk about this problem at the next ISA conference in Washington. SAR has asked me to make a presentation.

SUKA: Well, I'll see you there. I'm going too; someone I met at High Table the other month has asked me to give a talk, off-the-cuff stuff I think, on the developments in Eastern Europe in 1989. I won't have to write anything beforehand—you know the sort of thing, tell them all about how important history is and how they don't take a long enough view.

IRTS: No, I'd say that ...

SUKA: Let me finish. Those events really have made things difficult for you theorists, haven't they! I had to laugh as the Cold
War disappeared, thinking about how so many of you kept telling me about the importance of theory over the years. All that
stuff about bipolarity and multipolarity; never understood it
myself. It always struck me that you were all failed historians. It
seems to me that your intellectual credibility has been swept
away overnight. Mind you, I doubt that that will stop you. You'll
soon be turning out articles proving how the end of the Cold
War was always inevitable, a sort of systems transformation, I
suppose.

IRTS (*aware of a pending monologue*): Well, it looks as if the bathroom is now free. After you. I'll look out for you in Washington,
that is, if I can save enough to pay my airfare!

SUKA: See you there, but please don't try to sell me a theory!

Scene 2

*Washington, April 1990. The ISA conference. IRTS and SUKA are
drinking at the hotel bar when SAR, JUSOFS, WESTFEM, and
TSITSI approach.*

IRTS: Hello, or should I say "Hi?" I've been reading your papers for
tomorrow's panel. I guess I'm going to disagree with you. Your
North American bias is so evident. It's as if you're the first academic community to ask about the influences underlying your
research, and you really have this thing about decline. But remember that it was an Englishman—Paul Kennedy—who got
all your presidential candidates panicking about it back in '88.[1]
I had to smile when I saw that the "must-read" piece of '89, just
a year later, was Francis Fukuyama's "The End of History?"[2]

SUKA: I rather liked that—better than all that quantitative stuff.
And it's good to see Hegel back in fashion.

IRTS: Where was I? Ah yes, I was saying that you Americans go
from one extreme to the other. Mind you, I agree that the end of

the Cold War has provoked a real crisis of self-identity for the U.S. As Mick Cox has noted,[3] the Cold War was one continual system, detente notwithstanding, that not only managed U.S.-Soviet relations and relations within each alliance but also fundamentally structured and legitimized each superpower's domestic society. Now that all of that has disappeared, what will replace it as the organizing principle of international relations? Will you have to invent a new enemy—Japan maybe, or Islamic fundamentalism? More important, for me, what will this do to the future direction of international relations?

SAR: Come on, that's not fair. Your country has been just as involved as the U.S., if not more so, with maintaining the Cold War, and your Prime Minister Thatcher was more reluctant than anyone to let it pass away peacefully. Anyway, surely you'd agree there are new threats and new policy dilemmas? That isn't just a matter of U.S. bias, is it?

SUKA: I'm afraid it is, and it's always been that way. Take the development of the subject of international relations itself. It's always been dominated by American policy concerns and by the prevailing fashions and fads of U.S. academia.

IRTS: Come on, SUKA, that's a bit ethnocentric of you, isn't it? Remember how and where the subject started: It started as a separate discipline with the establishment of the first chair in the subject at Aberystwyth in 1919. British academics played a leading role in defining the content of the subject in those days, and in a way that had enormously damaging consequences for the establishment of a truly international discipline. They accepted the legitimacy of the Versailles settlement and shared a normative commitment to preventing war. Remember—they saw war from a liberal perspective and the First World War as a war that no one had wanted; in other words, as the result of misperception and misunderstanding.

SAR: Well, that is still a major theme in the subject, and it isn't ethnocentric in any way, is it?

IRTS: No, although much of the thinking about the subject has suffered from a terrible ethnocentrism, as Ken Booth has argued so persuasively with regards to strategy.[4] But the point I want to make about the idealists is that they rejected war as a rational instrument of statecraft, having seen the incredibly destructive effects of trench warfare, which led to more deaths amongst British troops before breakfast one morning in the Somme than the U.S. lost in the entire Vietnam War. All this for a few yards of mud in Flanders that would be regained by the other side in their next offensive. It's hardly surprising that the idealists wanted so much to prevent war. The problem was that they elevated the peaceful resolution of conflict to the main consideration of international relations without realizing that this peace was all right only as long as you were situated in one of the powers that had won the war and could accept the resulting order as just. So, right from the start, the subject was defined by its national setting.

SUKA: I agree with you, but my point is that the real spate of growth in the subject, which led to it having the contours it has today, was very much a U.S.-defined growth. I'm talking about Morgenthau and the realists ...

SAR: Most of whom emigrated from Europe in the 1930s, as a matter of fact; so much for your "American" dominance!

IRTS: Hang on. SUKA is correct in that realism was very much affected by the fact that the U.S. was the leading world power. First of all, realism justified the policy of containment and saw the Soviets as trying to maximize power. By the way, do you notice how Morgenthau seems to be silent over why such policies aren't guiding U.S. policy?! But the point is that realism was the intellectual framework for U.S. foreign policy. It also had the added advantage of a strong appeal to common sense: After the Holocaust and Stalin's purges, it was easy to believe in a concept of evil, or at least self-interested, human nature.

SUKA: Human nature—now there's a thing that hasn't changed in the history of international relations.

IRTS: Hang on, SUKA, let's not get into that debate. I want to make my point about why realism dominated in the U.S. Another reason was its claim to be objective; surely this approach appealed to a U.S. that had successfully applied the "sciences" of management and economics to dominate the world economy and the science of nuclear physics to unleash the powers of the natural world. The same principles could surely be applied to international politics, couldn't they? Anyway, Morgenthau really did try to sell his product as science. In this regard, by the way, I think that you were very mistaken, SAR, when you told JUSOFS that "realists in international relations do not practice science." Morgenthau had to claim that his approach was objective, and early in *Politics Among Nations* he very clearly set out the aim as being that of creating a science. It may not be your view of science, SAR, and I'll come to that later, but remember that his work was as much concerned with attacking the idealists as it was with creating an alternative.

SAR: Yes, but he ...

IRTS: Wait, let me note, finally, that realism emerged just as positivism was developing in the U.S. You can't separate the appeals of realism from the opportunities opened up by positivism. All in all, realism was deeply and profoundly affected by the fact that it developed in the U.S., just as Morgenthau himself was profoundly affected by the Weberian tradition from which he emerged.

SAR: That's too simplistic! As I said to JUSOFS, it was the lack of scientific rigor that I and others found so unacceptable. This "theory" was merely untestable assumptions dressed up as a theory, and it had strong normative elements. Fancy arguing that the motivation didn't matter; Snyder, Bruck, and Sapin really disposed of that argument.[5] The behavioral movement rejected realism completely.

SUKA: I rejected it, too, but for different reasons. The whole notion that you could uncover laws of international relations was ridiculous to me. I remember seeing the first edition of Morgenthau's book. Half of it was common sense, the rest seemed irrelevant. I agree with you, SAR, that ignoring motivations is unacceptable, but the Snyder framework didn't exactly help, did it?! I found it incomprehensible. And, it didn't exactly lead to a lot of case studies, did it? I think that there's no alter-

native but to study the individuals who make the decisions and
see why they decided what they did. That's scholarship—piec-
ing together the evidence about their motivations. The rest is
sheer irrelevancy. You can't construct theories about state behavior; they're all unique! Anyone for another drink?

IRTS: Hang on a minute. I want to get back to SAR's point. I cannot
believe that you really think that behavioralism was a distinctive theoretical enterprise. I find the brilliant exposé by
Vasquez totally convincing;[6] he showed that the behavioralist
movement accepted the three core assumptions of realism—
states as actors, the division between domestic and international societies, and the hierarchy of issues that gives priority to
military factors. All the behavioralists did was to operationalize
the realist paradigm. They never put forward a different theoretical position, only a methodological one. It was never more
than this, despite the heated debates between traditionalists
and scientists. Bull had much more in common with Kaplan
than the famous exchange suggested![7]

SUKA: Behavioralism! What a pretentious load of scientific rubbish. It was the American academic community trying to be as
respectable as their counterparts in the sciences; I mean the
proper sciences, or economics. I look back on that period as a
very sad one. What was the phrase? "If you can't measure it, it
doesn't exist." It amazes me just how much of a hold that approach had on the subject—and still has, in fact. Needless to
say, I don't read—if that is even the right word—the main U.S.
journals today. You need a degree in mathematics to understand the table of contents! I don't know which way up *ISQ*
should be held. Even worse, the "scientists" claim the discipline as their own. In fact, my guess is that the majority of IR
academics in the U.S. don't subscribe to behavioralism in any
guise. Just look at the best journals—*World Politics, Foreign Affairs,* and even that radical one—what's it called? Oh yes, *Foreign Policy.* Not many formulae in these, just good old-fash-
ioned historically informed scholarship.

SAR: No, that's wrong. No serious scholar I know still accepts the
simplistic and naive positivism that ruled the day in the 1950s

and 1960s. But I know that we had to go through that phase in order to get where we are today. It was a phase in the development of the social sciences, and we've now moved beyond it. In 1976, I myself wrote of the problems positivism had led to.[8]

JUSOFS: True, but you also proclaimed foreign policy analysis to be a "normal science" back in 1975 or '76,[9] didn't you?

SAR: I did, and now I know that claim was too optimistic. Yet I did feel for a while, back in the early 1970s, that we could do it, that we could create a Kuhnian normal science. I know now that's impossible, which is one reason why I'm so interested in the impact of national factors on the way the subject is studied— because maybe my earlier optimism reflected a distinctive U.S. experience. I'm very conscious of the message that you post-modernists and critical theorists keep sending me. That is why we're having this conversation; I want to understand where the subject is going.

IRTS: But to do that you have to see where it has come from. In my view of things, positivism still dominates IR in the U.S.A. SUKA is right, of course, in that many IR academics in North America distance themselves from the excesses of behavioralism and see themselves as operating within a very different methodology. But IR in its theoretical guise is absolutely shot through with positivistic assumptions about the relationship between evidence and theory. Your earlier conversation with JUSOFS showed that only too clearly, SAR. You think that dropping behavioralism and its quantitative excesses is enough. The trouble is that you still talk as if there is *a* world out there waiting to be discovered. It's as if you're trying to find your way across a landscape and all you need is a map, so you look at the ones in the IR store and find out which one covers the terrain that you're interested in.

SAR: That's old hat. Dave Singer used exactly that analogy in his level-of-analysis piece thirty years ago![10]

IRTS: No, you misunderstand the point. The point is that there isn't *a* map; social life isn't like that at all. The terrain of social life is distinctly different from that of geographical terrain; in social life there are *always* two distinct stories to tell, and there is no way of deciding between them.

SUKA: I know what you mean—or at least I think you mean the argument that statesmen ...

WESTFEM: You don't mean *just* states*men*, do you?

SUKA: Sorry, my dear, I don't quite get your point.

WESTFEM: I'm sure you don't.

SUKA: Anyway, to continue, the point is that statesmen are constrained by factors such as law, morality, ethics, and world opinion and they have to choose within these constraints. I remember that Bismarck once said ...

IRTS: No, no, no, you don't see my point at all. I mean that there are two distinct versions of social life, one stressing the explanation of behavior, the other stressing the understanding of it. Those who take the first view see individuals as having little choice given the fact that the society they're born into already has a moral code, social norms, and a language, all of which they learn through socialization. Those taking the latter view want to uncover the reasons actors give for their behavior; they see individuals as creating their world and, at the very least, as deciding how to interpret rules. These two accounts are distinct, mutually exclusive, and cannot be combined.

SUKA: I thought combining them was what social science was all about.

IRTS: Oh, you don't understand do you?! Anyway, then there is the separate but no less undecidable issue of what can broadly be seen as holism versus individualism, as the whole versus the parts. You can believe in any combination of these two sets of categories. That is to say, you can explain either top-down or bottom-up, or go in either way in the understanding mode. There is no way of combining the whole and the parts or deciding between them.

JUSOFS: This is what I've been telling SAR—that his categories of thought are so modernist.

IRTS: Well, can I say something about your own position ...

SUKA: No, wait a minute. I really cannot accept your preposterous view that there are *always* two stories to tell. That's ridiculous. A good historian can carefully balance the two sets and then present his findings to the scholarly community, who can then investigate whether he has misrepresented the evidence.

SAR: Hold it! I find myself at odds with all of you. I remember reading something by Anthony Giddens, something about the concept of structuration,[11] which offered a way of combining the two perspectives. And didn't Alex Wendt publish something in *IO* about this recently, applying it to IR?[12]

IRTS: Sure, I know Giddens's work, but he doesn't solve the problem; he merely redescribes it more fully. After all, how can you know when it is structure and when it's action? Who is the omniscient observer? Anyway, Giddens has to see structure as primary, given the way he formulates it. The bottom line here is that you all talk as if this were a methodological problem, or at worst an epistemological one. In fact, it's a fundamental ontological contradiction: Are individuals or structures accorded ontological primacy? My view is that there is no secure ground from which to make that decision. This makes positivism simply mistaken in its view of social life.

SAR: Oh, come on! No one thinks that there is simply a world of facts out there, do they?

SUKA: Well, as a matter of fact ...

SAR: You're kidding, aren't you?

IRTS: He isn't, I'm afraid. But the point is that you seem to think that the world is waiting to be discovered and that the reasons why facts aren't easily obtainable is because the theories we use are biased. Remove the bias, and we see the light of day more clearly. The problem with this view is that, since theories determine what counts as the facts, different theories cannot simply be assessed by the same set of evidence.

SAR: Could you elaborate on what you have in mind?

IRTS: Sure, take for example the current division in the subject between the competing paradigms—realism, neorealism, pluralism, and structuralism. Proponents of each simply disagree on
what the questions are, which means that they cannot share
the same pieces of evidence. Ask a pluralist, a structuralist, and
a neorealist who the main actors are, or what the main issues
are, and they'll have no basis for resolving any disputes that
arise. The real point here is that U.S. IR still goes on talking as if
knowledge is some kind of representation of reality, whereas it's
really an interpretation of it, and never complete at that. How
can it be? You can never decide whether a holist or individualist
approach is correct, since that distinction misunderstands the
role of theory. And remember, there are always two accounts
that can be told, one from the inside, stressing the actor's reasons for action; the other from the outside, focusing on the
causes of behavior.

SUKA: I think we're getting away from the point, which is the role
of national location in determining the content of IR.

WESTFEM: Well, actually, it isn't as simple as that, is it? Individuals
aren't just affected by their national location; there's also their
gender, which seems to get short shrift in this discussion. It's as
if gender were unimportant.

IRTS: I agree totally with you, and I want to say something about
that, but the reason for the absence of a feminist voice up to
now is that we've been discussing how IR *has* been studied.
Feminist approaches are very recent, and although they clearly
go straight to the heart of the assumptions surrounding the
content of IR, they simply weren't heard at all during the
periods we were discussing. And, by the way, national factors
are also augmented by class factors. I know that this notion
may seem very European, but class location really does affect
the way in which individuals study a subject.

WESTFEM (*staring in disbelief*): You sure are quick to move from
feminist concerns!

IRTS: No ... I ... I mean I just want to stress that people have different agendas. Take the four paradigms I mentioned. Note that

the one most concerned with economic factors has had very few adherents in the U.S., or the U.K. for that matter. Structuralism was developed in Latin America rather than North America. This had to be because the world is simply different there. They don't see bipolarity and the arms race as central issues in international relations; they are more concerned with core-periphery relationships in international economics. In the U.S. IR community, there's still a marked resistance to economic theories, especially anything that smacks of Marxism. It's almost as if it is methodologically unacceptable. As JUSOFS pointed out in his earlier discussion with you, SAR, Marxism offends the "rules of scholarship" laid down by positivism. After all, you can't always see, touch, feel, or measure structures. You have to infer their existence as the best explanation, and that offends even the most enlightened neopositivist.

SAR: I hear you, but you know as well as I do that economic theories can't explain all foreign policy behavior.

IRTS: Yes, but note the importance of the boundaries you are constructing by your definition. Why states as actors? Don't you see that state boundaries may be totally unimportant to those starving in Ethiopia; your division of the world into the actors and the "relevant" processes is a remarkably important act of power. The world you see is the world as it appears to someone of your gender, class, and age living in *the* superpower. It isn't that your view is wrong or too comfortable, it's just that it becomes tempting to define *the* subject in that way. There are other realities out there, and at its simplest and most innocent level your view is bound to reflect the set of salient policy concerns for your own country. For one obvious reason, your newspapers will cover events that are presumed to be of interest to the readers, which have to reflect the things that affect them most. Reporters may even write the stories in a way that supports U.S. interests; I know virtually all the journalists in Britain write their stories with a clear eye on British concerns, and that's apart from the vexing issue of whether they take the government's view of things.

SAR: They're worried about being relevant in my country, too.

IRTS: That leads me to my next point. Take the problem of policy relevance. Now, SAR, I know that you have never been one to try and get your ideas into policy circles, trying, as it were, to whisper advice to the prince. But far too many of your colleagues do. Sure, it happens in Britain too, but the amount of movement between academia and government service is far lower in Britain than in the U.S. Of course, often it's those who are most vigorous in attacking the role of theory who seek to convince those in governments that they have some kind of "understanding" and "independence" that allows them to "speak truth to power." I always thought that this sounded rather like they had a theory! If not, I don't see why governments should listen to them.

SAR: It's not clear that they do, except perhaps at lower levels of the bureaucracy.

IRTS: But, that is a diversion. The point I'm trying to make is that studying IR in the U.S. must affect your view of what are the dominant issues, and much more important, it must affect the mind-set that determines what you will accept as a good explanation of events. By this I mean that professional standards of the IR community in the U.S.A. are something that you have to work within. You can hardly challenge them. Look how difficult it is to publish material in the main journals if that material does not fit in with the dominant paradigms and, more subtly, the dominant epistemological and methodological assumptions. Why is it, do you think, that in the 1980s the British journal *Millennium* has published what have been viewed later as major pieces? The answer is that U.S. journals were not receptive to them. This is clearest in the case of critical theory, postmodernism, and, most recently, feminist theory. In each case a British, student-run journal has published landmark pieces. Isn't it ridiculous that the journal's special issue on women and IR[13] was the first such collection in "malestream" IR, even though feminist theory has been established for far longer in the U.S. than in the U.K.?

SAR: Well, I've published in that journal, too. I guess the reason it has been so innovative is that it's willing to encourage people to think innovatively, without expecting the same criteria of scholarship as you find in the main U.S. journals. But, IRTS, you'd have to admit that many of the British journals tend to be very unexciting, with little theoretical innovation from non-U.S. scholars.

IRTS: The main point I want to make is that the subject has been dominated by U.S. academics and therefore by an agenda that reflects U.S. policy concerns.

SAR: But it has always been open to you to reject that agenda and put forward alternatives; we've been disappointed that you haven't done more in this regard.

SUKA: If you ask me, too many of our academics have spent too much time chasing U.S. theories and trying to apply them to Britain. Most of them don't fit at all. Take bureaucratic politics; the literature on this subject applies only to the U.S. and its specific system of foreign policy decisionmaking. To say nothing of all that comparative foreign policy data stuff, what is it Crayon or ...

SAR: Actually it's CREON ...

SUKA: Sorry, thought you were meant to color in the boxes. Anyone for another drink?

IRTS: But, SAR, you miss the point again. It isn't simply that U.S. policy concerns have dominated the agenda of IR; it's much deeper than that. I mean, let there be no doubt, I totally believe that what was happening to the U.S. at any given time had a massive effect on what U.S. IR scholars were doing. It could be simply because that was what they thought they had to think about and explain, or because their chance to have an impact on policy depended on how well they addressed the agenda defined as being policy-relevant, or because addressing that agenda was the best way of getting research grants.

SAR: Sure, I've often commented on that.

IRTS: I know, but if you trace the history of IR since 1945 it's literally amazing to note just how much the theoretical agenda has been driven by the U.S. policy agenda. Let me just give you a few random examples: Think of the whole emphasis of the strategic and defense studies literature on crisis management, and the way that ethnocentrism has pervaded the U.S. strategic studies literature. Think of the work on polarity theories in the 1960s, just as U.S. politicians thought about the effects of the Sino-Soviet split. Think of the bureaucratic politics literature and how it was influenced by the perceived need to explain how the Vietnam quagmire occurred. Think of the IPE literature of the 1970s and 80s, entirely driven by notions of hegemonic stability and regimes, and all related to the changing position of the U.S. economy in that period. Think of the literature on interdependence, modernization, and transnationalism, all presented as theories of IR but based on the U.S. experience of the late 60s and early 70s. You'd think that no one else had come across nonstate actors, or that European economic integration hadn't occurred. Finally, think of the rise of neorealism.

JUSOFS: Which neorealism do you have in mind?

IRTS: Well, in both its military-political guise—that is, as in Waltz and Gilpin—and in its economic guise—as in Krasner and Keohane. Both versions are intimately linked to the domestic and foreign policy experiences of the U.S. in the late 70s. There are loads of other examples, but the point is simply that the subject has been so dominated by the U.S. academic community that U.S. policy concerns have become those of the profession.

SAR: I think you ...

IRTS: And it's also true that the dominant U.S. theories have become intrenched as *the* theory of IR. As Stanley Hoffmann has noted, IR is an American social science. Yet U.S. scholars have persisted in decrying Soviet IR theory as clearly bogus because it's designed to serve the interests of the Soviet leadership. What's the difference?

SAR: There is one massive difference, and well you know it. You are free to challenge our theories, and you have done so yourself. I can't help wondering why on earth you don't come up with some of your own rather than moan about our work. I can take criticism as much as the next person. In fact, I've welcomed it throughout my career, but you've got to do something positive, not merely sit on the sidelines and criticize.

SUKA: I keep telling him that. Stop testing these stupid U.S. theories and get on with some real IR scholarship.

IRTS: But you don't see, do you, how difficult it is to create alternatives? The U.S. IR profession dominates the world IR community in so many ways. You have so much more in the way of resources; you have so many people working in the area; you publish nearly all of the major journals—and that is an interesting point, because the journals are major precisely because you know that your peers rate them highly, or at least read them. How many of your libraries take the leading British journals, *Review of International Studies,* the BISA house journal, or *Millennium*? Let me tell you: The *Review* had, when it recently changed publishers, less than fifty U.S. subscriptions. Yet if you go to any U.K. college library, the chances are that it will have a large percentage of *your* main journals, certainly *Foreign Affairs, Foreign Policy, International Security, International Organization, ISQ, World Politics,* and *Alternatives,* to name just the most obvious.

SAR: I don't see what effect this has on scholarship.

IRTS: It means that you won't publish in our journals because you don't think it will help with tenure or professional reputation. Conversely, we have to keep up with your journals because we know that's where the main pieces will appear. The same thing applies to books. How many of the U.S. IR community know as much about the main texts and monographs published in the U.K. as their U.K. counterparts know about the U.S. literature? How many U.K. or, heaven forbid, French or German texts get adopted in U.S. universities? Then, remember the size of the respective academic communities: How many universities teach IR in the U.S.—100, 200, 300? In the U.K., we have probably no more than thirty-five institutions teaching any IR, and U.K. colleges are very small, with maybe an average of 4,500 students each. So, not surprisingly, the sales of books are very low in the U.K. and text publishing is absolutely dwarfed by the U.S. literature.

SAR: Stop, you're making my heart bleed. I can't help it if your government only sends, what, a quarter as many students on to college as in the U.S.; but I take your point.

IRTS: I'm not trying to say how bad it is in the U.K. as much as I'm trying to point out how unique the U.S. is. If it's bad in the U.K., which is the second main IR community, I suppose, what must it be like elsewhere? Serious U.K. academics have little choice but to follow the lead of the U.S. community because that community's voice dominates the entire profession. To be taken seriously means that you have to address the contents of *ISQ* or *IO*; it isn't enough to know only what is in the *Review* or *Millennium*. All of these factors make it impossible to talk of a neutral or even a universally applicable discipline. I don't mean that there can be no theoretical exchange. Of course, there is a lot of truly inter-national work; but the sheer size of the U.S. community is really important in determining what counts as good IR. It's a bit like the national interest; it's a term that the government gets to define, but defining the language of debate allocates power.

JUSOFS: All this is music to my ears. I agree with everything you are saying. But surely you'd agree that the postpositivist movement is breaking down all these boundaries and patterns of dominance.

SUKA: I think they are breaking down the standards of good scholarship; it all started in France you know …

IRTS: Look, I totally support the aims of the postpositivist movement, but I have to enter two main reservations. The first is that I want to know why the approaches have taken off in the U.S. in the middle to late 1980s, when they have been around for at least twenty years and popular in the social sciences for a good decade and a half. I find something rather intriguing about that question; why should mainly white, mainly male, mainly middle-class scholars in the most wealthy country of the world turn to these approaches?

JUSOFS: I think that neorealism had a lot to do with it; people got very dissatisfied with that retreat to what Robert Cox has called "problem-solving" theory.[14]

IRTS: Yes, but he also said that all theory is for some purpose, that it serves some interests. So, I can't help but ask what purpose is postpositivism serving?

SUKA: Getting tenure, I suspect. It's really effective; all you do is write in such a way that no one can understand a word and two things happen; people think you must be brilliant, because they can't understand it, and then a group of you get together and cite one another, publish one another, and generally praise each other. It's an industry, but spare a thought for all those trees in Newfoundland that are felled to print the pages and pages of the books and journals. Is it worth all those trees?

IRTS: I don't agree with that at all, although I know it's a common response. But I want to make my second point. This is that poststructuralism, or postmodernism, or whatever you call it, has a really damning set of problems. I don't want to bore you with them, as you all know them, but let me just list the main ones.

SUKA: When I hear the word postmodernism, I reach for my revolver!

IRTS: I'll ignore that. The main problem I see is that the postmodernism of Barthes, Foucault, and Derrida is unavoidably relativistic. That may be fine in literature, art, or architecture, but it certainly isn't in social life. I don't like the idea that the voice of the beaten woman or the abused child is merely one amongst several interpretations, with no one having any greater claim for being heard or accepted. I know the arguments for methodological pluralism, or whatever Richard Rorty's phrase is, but I honestly believe that postmodernism is unavoidably relativistic. I guess that puts me at odds with both WESTFEM and JUSOFS, but I want to make that worry clear.

WESTFEM: Well, I certainly have a problem with your claim that postmodernism is relativistic; after all, where would that leave feminist postmodernists?

IRTS: I was going on to say something about that. My second point is that postmodernism is apolitical. It says only "resist," but resist what? It rejects all forms of domination, yet seems almost nihilistic. You all know that it has been severely attacked for being the new conservatism, and I must say that this worries me. I know you've written widely on this, WESTFEM, but I think that the absence of *a* standpoint really causes problems. In that light I agreed with Bob Keohane when he called feminist postmodernism an oxymoron.[15]

WESTFEM: But he attacked the wrong target. Most of us now see ourselves as postmodern feminists, not as feminist postmodernists.

SUKA: I don't believe this. What on earth does that mean? I'll have to go to the bathroom!

(*SUKA exits.*)

IRTS: I'm sorry, WESTFEM. My final point is that there is a whole list of other minor problems: the lack of a transcendental subject; the resultant difficulty of developing notions of intersubjectivity; the logical problems this leads to in constructing a notion of a society; the absence of a way of explaining how discourses come into existence and change; the lack of any account of why some social forces dominate. I could go on, but let me conclude with what I consider the central issue—that we have to distinguish between critical theory and postmodernism. I know that it's all confusing because the same people seem to have progressed in the past decade from the former to the latter, but the distinction is absolutely vital. Critical theory, given its quasi-Marxist origins, does adopt a standpoint. It doesn't deny the linkage between knowledge and power; indeed, that is its central theme. But it does have a view of emancipatory theory, which can both be distinguished from the relativistic impulses of postmodernism and allows critical theory to distance itself from problem-solving theory. In this sense, Foucault and Habermas are saying very different things, and it's a mistake to lump them together. I see critical theory as genuinely capable of extending IR by showing the ways in which knowledge serves the interests of power, whereas my worry is that postmodernism will never be taken seriously, that it will drag down with it the whole attempt to undermine the positivistic dominance of the subject. I guess I agree with Fred Halliday when he calls postmodernism an "idealist evasion."[16] I'm also sure that TSITSI cannot possibly accept such a relativistic version of feminism as WESTFEM proposes when she talks of embracing postmodernism.

SUKA (*returning*): This is all irrelevant, IRTS. You've been lecturing us for too long. I think that if this is what IR is going to be in the future, then I ought to retire or join the history department.

IRTS: Wait a second. Before you all go, can I ask you, WESTFEM, and you, TSITSI, one question? I really do welcome—although that immediately smacks of patronizing—the introduction of feminist perspectives into IR, and I hope that it does move beyond the "women and" phase; but I wonder what you think feminist theories of IR should do. I ask this precisely because it's a question that bothers me. Should they address the "malestream" agenda? Surely not, since this approach would merely be the equivalent of "add women and stir." But if they try to address another agenda, won't they be marginalized or dismissed as irrelevant, as not doing "real" IR, which I freely admit means "male" IR? Isn't this a dilemma, and isn't it one that must divide women according to class and national setting? Can we get together and talk about this again? I fear I've said far too much and silenced other voices, but the issue really does matter if we're going to be a reflective and self-conscious discipline.

SAR: Well, at least none of us seems to agree with anyone else on every issue. Is this a healthy sign?

JUSOFS: I'd like a chance to reply to IRTS; I think you misunderstand postmodernism.

WESTFEM: And I think you oversimplify my position, but I agree we ought to talk more.

SUKA: Personally, I think Gorbymania has gone to all your heads. What we need is a return to the good old, bad old days of the

Cold War. That would stop all this rubbish about postmodernism and feminism; then we could get back to the real agenda of
IR—war, alliances, you know. Anyway, does anyone know
where the bathroom is? I hope I don't have to queue, or given
what we've been talking about, I guess I should say stand in
line.

IRTS: Oh, SAR, can I just have a word with you about something
else? You're on the ISA Governing Council, aren't you? Well, I
want you to help BISA and the other national IR associations.
Apparently, ISA has decided that it is *the* ISA and that the other
national associations are affiliated with it. We in BISA got a letter last year demanding that we send in our report, or else we'd
be expelled. I know it's not meant to look like American hegemony, but some people could get the wrong idea.

Scene 3

It is the early 1990s. IRTS is in his office talking to SUKA.

SUKA: We're all asking the same question, so I have to ask you.
What have recent events done to your thinking about our field?
Have you had to readjust your theories? Or are they still intact?
I'll tell you what I think: Your theories have been exposed as
worthless. The theoretical emperor has no clothes. You didn't
predict the end of communism, and you told me on the plane
over to the ISA conference last year that the world had seen the
end of power politics. I told you then that human nature was
unchanging and that you'd do better to learn the lessons of history. I told my students that communism would collapse as far
back as the early 1960s, when I first started teaching. I was
right, you see, whereas you kept telling me that bipolarity was
stable. You kept quoting someone called Waltz.

IRTS: Hang on a minute. You may have predicted the decline of
communism, but you saw its inevitable decline in everything
that happened. And you predicted, on numerous TV and radio
programs, any number of wars and coups that never happened. Just face it, SUKA, you have a fixed view of the world.
You see all the recent events as altering nothing. I heard you on

the BBC the other day warning about the rise of nationalism in Eastern Europe, saying that it would be the cause of war in the future.

SUKA: Of course I said that. I believe it. Human nature hasn't changed, and nothing you can say will convince me otherwise. Look at Saddam Hussein. He's the latest in a line of despots and megalomaniacs stretching back throughout history. He rose like them, ruled like them, and will fall like them. Nothing has changed since Thucydides wrote. Human nature is fixed, and we have to start from there. I have to tell you, I laughed my head off when I heard all you "experts" explaining how the Gulf War started. You resorted to the kind of theories and accounts that you've spent your career denouncing. If old Morgenthau could see you now! All of you who wrote about how his view of people was outmoded, who scored easy points in trivial articles and in easy conference settings—wasn't he justified by the Gulf War, wasn't it a classic realist confrontation? How else do you explain the regional balance of power or the foreign policy of Jordan? As for the U.S. leadership, well, it was just the war they needed to regain their status in the world.

IRTS: I couldn't disagree with you more. The Gulf War couldn't be explained by the realist position; to explain it, you need to get inside the heads of the actors and see how Saddam, and Bush, Thatcher, Major, and the rest, defined the problem. But tell me, do you really think that the war could have happened in the bad old days of bipolarity? Wouldn't the Soviets have either prevented agreement at the UN or put pressure on Saddam to stop the invasion of Kuwait? Surely the war was possible only because of the changes in the structure of the system.

SUKA: Oh stop it, you're making me sick. You speak of international relations as if it's some impersonal mechanism with power flowing around in it like the liquid in a hydraulic brake system. In your view of politics, and of life, too, there's no role for individuals, and there's nothing to teach our students. What's the point of IR if we can't show our students how to learn from history?

IRTS: But what lessons from what history? You always talk of the world as if it's immediately and unproblematically available to you, as if there is just one world about which true statements can be made.

SUKA: That's exactly what I believe. Of course you have to follow the rules of scholarship and get into the mind of the man you're looking at, but that's what an education in IR should give students. Not all this mathematical rubbish you see in *ISQ* and the like. What on earth does that have to do with scholarship? It has more to do with getting tenure, if you ask me; all you need to do is publish a few tedious, safe articles expanding the "research paradigm" incrementally, and you're in, you're one of the intellectual leaders of an approach or method. Pretty pictures, graphs, matrixes, and numbers are fine in science, but they have absolutely nothing to do with the reality of international relations. My god, these approaches continue to discipline the discipline, and the real-world questions of morality, and, dare I say it, right and wrong, get left out of the discussion. I remember old SAR saying at a seminar years ago that he was trying to be value-free. How ridiculous! Teaching involves judgments and they have to relate to values.

IRTS: I have to interrupt. SAR, like most of his colleagues, although not all by any means, has moved on. He's still learning and thinking, which is more than can be said for a lot of people in Britain. Most IR here still seems to regard Morgenthau as a bit too modern. You yourself seem to quote Morgenthau as if he were the last word in IR theory.

SUKA: Well, I certainly think that IR hasn't advanced since Morgenthau, and even Morgenthau goes too far in seeing forces and structures at work. He is really a bit too structural and deterministic for my liking.

IRTS: I think you're really badly out of date. There's some excellent work going on in IR in many different countries, and it's a massive advance on realism.

SUKA: Fine. I'm sure it has some excellent mathematical insights. But tell me this: What do these new theories tell us about the Gulf War? Go on, answer me; tell me what postmodernists or feminists can tell us about the war. Or is it that they can't say anything about the real world? By the way, do you know that we had our first paper on feminist theory at a BISA conference this year? They can't say we're behind the times now, can they?

IRTS: That's very complacent of you. The 1991 ISA conference had about twenty-eight papers on feminist theory, and they've been having them for several years. We are many years behind, as always. Anyway, you know only too well that the challenge of the postmodernists and feminists is much greater than merely trying to answer questions on your, or more accurately, the orthodoxy's agenda. That is what's wrong with Keohane's acceptance of the feminist standpoint position; it can add new things to the existing agenda. I think that feminists, like postmodernists and critical theorists, are trying to do something much more radical, something that guarantees that they will not fit easily into the existing agenda, where they would otherwise be marginalized. As I see it, and I wish WESTFEM and TSITSI were here to comment on this, postmodernists and feminists are challenging what gets accepted as the real world. They show only too clearly that the subject of IR helps to perpetuate the status quo, or, to use your words, the real world. I think that the critical voices are raising absolutely vital issues—look at Cynthia Enloe's superb analysis of what you call the real world.[17]

SUKA: I heard about that book. It has nothing to do with the real subject of IR.

IRTS: By the way, I had a fax the other day from JUSOFS asking me if I'd take part in a colloquium at the next ISA. It's on the topic of postmodernism and the Gulf War. I don't know what to do. After all, the war caused a real argument on the Left in Britain, and I don't know how the postmodernists dealt with it in the U.S. I wouldn't want to go there and sound critical, but here, they suffered enormously from the charge of relativism after they attacked those on the Left who supported the war. I know of key left-wing writers who publicly supported the war who were then savaged for so doing. Most postmodernists at my institution spent their time showing that Bush or Major was just as bad as Saddam. I even had to give a presentation at one of their seminars at which the whole war was looked upon as a visual image. It really worried me. It smacked of apoliticism, and I found it all rather misplaced cultural relativism. The war wasn't a text, and real moral questions were involved. I fail to see how I can approach these matters without some moral or ethical foundations. So I'd better not go to the ISA.

SUKA: I wouldn't bother anyway. All these new theories—they're just fads; they're like a London bus. If you miss one, don't worry, another one will be along in five minutes. My god, if I spent the time necessary to catch up on the latest fads and fashions coming out of the U.S., I'd never do any real work. I'd have to read all these long-discredited German scholars, and then find that the fashion had changed and I now had to learn what some French bunch were saying. It's better not to bother in the first place. As I said earlier, the theory of IR is the same as it has always been. Don't be a dedicated follower of fashion, my boy. Do some real work. Go to the Public Records Office in London; that is where you go for scholarship, not to an ISA conference.

IRTS: I happen to get a lot out of an ISA conference.

SUKA: Rubbish. At ISA it's all networking, suits, power breakfasts, and self-defense mechanisms. The art of giving a paper at the ISA is to put up the sandbags as soon as you can; you know, protect yourself from any possible thought that you might say anything new or controversial and, most important, cover yourself with famous names—as in "My position here is basically that of Keohane, although I accept Grieco's critique, but as Krasner says ... etc." Better still, use these authors' first names—that implies that you know them. Wait, even better, use their nicknames. That's the real key to sandbagging, as in "I was talking to Chuck (they're all called Chuck) Hermann the other day and he told me that Ole and Jim were really impressed with what Tom was doing up at USC." See, it's easy. There's safety in numbers and in these particular names; they're like a wagon train drawn round you for when the Indians attack. Attack you, and they're attacking these people. No, don't go to ISA, unless you want a job in the states, in which case remember to praise everyone.

IRTS: You are really cynical, aren't you? You also fail to note how the "old boy" network works over here. It's just the same; you're either inside or outside the charmed circle, and it doesn't matter which academic community you're in. I think that's one of the most depressing features of the academic world. Whatever the subject or approach, there's always a hierarchy, always an orthodoxy. It's just more depressing when this feature recurs with the "new" approaches. But, having said all this, I still prefer the U.S. community. It's genuinely pluralistic, and there are several orthodoxies. In Britain there is really only one orthodoxy and all alternatives are looked down on. Moreover, in the U.S., at least they take theory seriously. More important, they don't treat their academics as badly as they do here, in terms of salary and research support. This month we've been asked to stop using headed stationery because we've run out of money. The point is that, for me, the U.S. IR scene is the only game in town. That is where the bulk of world IR gets done, and like it or not, we all have to respond to that agenda. It's like the "real" world of politics you talk about. We are to U.S. IR as Major is to Bush. Put "Discuss" after that sentence, and it would make a great exam question.

SUKA: I told SAR that at the ISA. I'm glad you agree with me on something.

IRTS: Well, only to a point. As I see it, the only problem is that the U.S. academic community doesn't seem to realize that they do dominate the discipline so much. Take the September 1990 issue of *ISQ*; it was a special issue entitled "Speaking the Language of Exile: Dissidence in International Studies."[18] What gets me about that special issue is not only that it ignores feminism—and that is a really worrying thought; as a friend of mine in feminist theory put it, "The old lefties are the worst"—but note that it talks about postmodernism and the like as being voices from exile. Now, exile has always been something rather nasty, something imposed and involving serious problems for the person put into exile. These dissident voices are not in exile; they're in universities in the wealthiest parts of the world. You see, even in the area of dissident voices, the U.S. still dominates. I wonder what TSITSI thinks of all this.

SUKA: Never mind. The U.S. dominance will end as soon as the U.S. ceases to dominate the real world of international relations! When are American soothsayers now forecasting that to occur? What is the current "must read" of the chattering classes in Washington? Some book forecasting the coming war with Japan.[19] So don't worry, IRTS, your fears about U.S. dominance will soon be over. We can then, according to your version of events, start learning the Japanese version of IR.

IRTS: Don't be so sarcastic. The U.S. is the only superpower and will remain so. The decline of the Soviet Union, and the end of the Cold War, gives IR theory a chance to become less dominated by U.S. policy concerns because it removes all the old certainties and parameters. My worry is that U.S. IR will go on addressing the U.S. foreign policy agenda anyway, just as it has done since 1945, and that even the critical voices will be led from U.S. universities. The alternatives will be outlined in the U.S. simply because of its relative size in the world IR community. You see, even in that *ISQ* special issue, exile was defined within a North American context. I'm reminded of the title of a Rolling Stones album from the early 1970s: If they are in exile, it's "Exile on Main Street."

SUKA: I recall that ...

IRTS: Anyway, I have to go and give a lecture now; it's on the topic of the "Special Relationship." I wonder if that special relationship between the U.S. and the U.K. applies as much in the academic world as they say it does in the "real" world. Or is it simply that we are two countries divided by a common language? Maybe IR is a subject divided by a common set of concepts; perhaps all IR books and journals, wherever published, should be stamped "Made in the U.S.A."

SUKA: Don't you mean what that Springsteen fellow used to yell out, "Bored by the U.S.A."? I'm off to have a cup of tea. All this theory leaves me feeling quite alienated. Why can't we just take the world as we find it and not try to dress everything in theory?

IRTS: Discuss!

ACT IV

Fathers (and Sons),
Mother Courage (and Her Children),
and the Dog, the Cave, and the Beef

James Der Derian

Prologue

Ever since the Sophists ran circles around Socrates, Plato and his followers have sought revenge by staging the triumph of reason over rhetoric. The practice persists: Nearly all students of political science cut their theory teeth on the Socratic dialogues, a practice that gives them a good start in the Western tradition of what the French literary critic Jacques Derrida referred to in *Of Grammatology* as *logocentrism*, the metaphysical conceit that the spoken word is closer to reality, always prior to and therefore more authentic than the written word.[1] But it is in a later work, *The Post Card: From Socrates to Freud and Beyond*, that, inspired by his discovery in Oxford's Bodleian Library of a postcard reproduction of a thirteenth-century illustration that shows Socrates at a table *writing* while Plato directs him from behind, Derrida addressed the distance between the writer, speaker, and reader. He reverses the modernist proclivity for the instructive dialogue in a deconstructive reading of what he calls "[P]lato's dream: To make Socrates write, and to make him write what he wants, his last command, *his will*. *To make* him write what he wants by letting him write what he wants."[2] In effect, Derrida sends the postcard back to the original writer, stamped address unknown, message untraceable, destiny forgotten.

Honored by Jim Rosenau's invitation to engage in a dialogue on the state of international relations theory—and weary of the polemics that only serve to sustain the exclusionary borders of that fictionally sovereign state—I weighed the epistemological costs of an *ersatz* dialogue against the didactic (not to mention, of course, careerist) opportunities of a response. Not all considerations were intellectual or professional. Would it be possible to respond in kind—and still be kind? Were the differences in approach too wide, the prehistory of the debate too nasty?

Let us first look at the most obvious difference, that between generations. Rosenau's dual intention in Act I—with a dialogue form as his vehicle—is to preempt criticisms that "superpower" social science cannot avoid a national bias by taking some critical first steps toward the formation of a more global yet less hegemonic social science. Here Rosenau certainly deserves credit for rejecting the easier form of polemical solo in favor of a more difficult—and much more entertaining—pas de deux between a "Senior American Scholar" and a "Junior U.S. or Foreign Scholar." (Should we assume from the difference in titles that Junior, state-bounded, will someday grow into Senior's continental status?) Rosenau might be surprised to learn in this regard that he shares common ground with the "mature" Foucault, who in one of his final interviews eloquently stated his preference for dialogue over against polemic:

> Questions and answers depend on a game—a game that is at once pleasant and difficult—in which each of the two partners takes pains to use only the rights given him by the other and by the accepted form of the dialogue. The polemicist, on the other hand, proceeds encased in privileges that he possesses in advance and will never agree to question. On principle, he possesses rights authorizing him to wage war and making that struggle a just undertaking; the person he confronts is not a partner in the search for the truth, but an adversary, an enemy who is wrong, who is harmful and whose very existence constitutes a threat. For him, then, the game does not consist of recognizing this person as a subject having the right to speak, but of abolishing him, as the interlocutor, from any possible dialogue; and his final objective will be, not to come as close as possible to a difficult truth, but to bring about

the triumph of the just cause he has been manifestly upholding from the beginning.[3]

In intention, at least, Rosenau presents us with a conversation rather than a contest. In execution, however, the exchange between SAR and JUSOFS is a dialogue only in a formal sense, containing all kinds of double-talk and monological reasoning. Neither of Rosenau's characters wins or loses in the conventional sense; nor do they, however, seem to gain or contribute new insights in the exchange. Instead of negotiating their differences, they scuttle sideways, like two crabs relying on first claw and then shell to protect their sovereign territories. They leave the cafeteria with their one-dimensional identities intact, each seeing in the other either a condescending old duffer or an impudent young Turk.

Fine criticisms, but as the elder spokesperson (no ageism or sexism here) would probably say, put up or shut up; which is, of course, yet another arbitrary delimitation of intellectual options—but one nonetheless with a pragmatic, injunctive power. Still, to reply in kind with a "dialogue"—or to rebut with an unkind polemic—would probably only serve to rigidify the extant borders of both IR and world politics. How, then, to open up Rosenau's formative dialogue to a supplementary reading without making deceptive moves to transcend or negate it? The best option, I believe, is to apply the insights of Mikhail Bakhtin's intertextual theory of *dialogism*, which shows how all understanding, like language itself, is a responsive act that depends upon prior discourses as well as anticipating future ones.[4] Since it is through the communicative acts of negotiating meaning and values with others that the self is constituted, identity *requires* difference: "[T]he psyche," says Bakhtin, "enjoys extraterritorial status."[5]

Yet, in world politics, the self clearly "enjoys" territorial and sovereign protection. This can partially be explained by the heightened sense of insecurity and long history of estrangement that have created 'deep identities' and a rationalist faith in the state to keep the contingencies of life at bay. These artesian sources of monological, sovereign reasoning in IR, which bubble up just when global dangers threaten to overcome the abilities of the nation-state to control them, induce a self-fulfilling dread and denial of an extraterritorial identity.[6]

In this context, consider first Bakhtin's critique of monologism:

> Ultimately, *monologism* denies that there exists outside of it another consciousness, with the same rights, and capable of responding on an equal footing, another and equal *I (thou)*. The monologue is accomplished and deaf to the other's response; it does not await it and does not grant it any *decisive* force. Monologue makes do without the other; that is why to some extent it objectivizes all reality. Monologue pretends to be the *last word*.[7]

And then the last words of Bakhtin, written in 1974:

> There is no first or last discourse, and dialogical context knows no limits (it disappears into an unlimited past and in our unlimited future). Even *past* meanings, that is those that have arisen in the dialogue of past centuries, can never be stable (completed once and for all, finished), they will always change (renewing themselves) in the course of the dialogue's subsequent development, and yet to come. At every moment of the dialogue, there are immense and unlimited masses of forgotten meanings, but, in some subsequent moments, as the dialogue moves forward, they will return to memory and live in renewed form (in a new context). Nothing is absolutely dead: every meaning will celebrate its rebirth.[8]

I believe Bakhtin's distinction provides a particularly apt exposé of what passes for criticism and debate in both Rosenau's dialogue and in the field of IR in general. Many might find fault with Rosenau's dialogue for leaving out particular voices: that of the woman, the third world thinker, the long-wave enthusiast, ad nauseum. In contrast, I (and others who have been lumped together as poststructuralist thinkers) would target Rosenau's construction of opposites—war/peace, male/female, domestic/international, objective/subjective—to define the phenomena and delimit the possibilities of IR. This criticism would also call into question the teleological claims (sometimes explicit but more often implicit) that some spiritual, revolutionary, or scientific process is at work to transcend, overcome, or rationalize these harmful binary oppositions. The aim is to study the powers behind the construction and enforcement of such oppositions and to understand how it is the "space between" rather than the binary units themselves that matter most in IR.[9]

Language, then, is the model: Our efforts to fix the meaning of what something is by establishing what it is not is always already warped by the space between sender and receiver, sign and referent, *langue* (the social code) and *parole* (individual message), author and reader. The heteroglossia of language—the constant renegotiation of meaning and values that goes on with each utterance—bespeaks a heterodoxia in world politics where radical alterity should be assumed and asserted rather than subsumed and repressed. These strategies shift if not obliterate Rosenau's seemingly natural (that is, necessary) fact-value dichotomy in which the anguished social scientist seeks to expunge subjective factors from his objective analysis.

In short, the goal should not and cannot be a single identity or grand theory for IR, be it in the formation of SAR's global social science or the end result of JUSOFS' marxoid dialectic. The aim is to live with and recognize the very *necessity* of heterogeneity for understanding ourselves and others. Paul de Man, in his exposition of Bakhtin's principle of *exotopy*, made this point with a high level of sophistication:

> On the other hand, dialogism also functions ... as a principle of radical otherness. ... [F]ar from aspiring to the telos of a synthesis or a resolution, as could be said to be the case in dialectical systems, the function of dialogism is to sustain and think through the radical exteriority or heterogeneity of one voice with regard to any other ... The self-reflexive, autotelic or, if you wish, narcissistic structure of form, as a definitional description enclosed with specific borderlines, is hereby replaced by an *assertion* of the otherness of the other, preliminary to even the possibility of a *recognition* of his otherness.[10]

A dialogical reading of Rosenau raises several questions. Is it possible to imagine and construct such a dialogue between SAR and JUSOFS in which their identities are not predetermined or fixed by national, class, or chronological origins external to the dialogue but constantly interacting and shifting in the interlocutionary space between the self and the other? Informed by this psychic interdependency, would such characters be less willing, perhaps even unable, to declare the other persona non grata in this extraterritorial land? In this move from a metalinguistic concept to an interdiscursive relationship, does dialogism exceed its function as a metaphor or formal model and point the way toward a re-formation of IR? Ultimately, the answer probably depends most on just how jealous each is of the right to the last word.

What follows is my effort to construct a hybrid dialogue that takes into account these concerns. Yes, it is overly self-conscious and predictably self-serving; but, as compensation and consolation, it is always aware—and celebratory—of the always absent other that evades the enclosure acts of this and other dialogues in IR.

Scene 1
Fathers (and Sons): The Formation of Orthodoxy in IR

(*A dialogue heard from behind the curtain.*)

"A Nihilist," his father said slowly. "As far as I can judge, that must be a word derived form the Latin *nihil—nothing*; the term must therefore signify a man who ... will admit nothing?"

"Better still, a man who will respect nothing," Paul Petrovich interjected, and then resumed his buttering.

"Who looks at everything critically," Arcady remarked.

"And what is the difference?" his uncle inquired.

"There is a difference. A Nihilist is a man who admits no established authorities, who takes no principles for granted, however much they may be respected."

"Well then? Is that a good thing?" his uncle interrupted.

"That depends on the circumstances, Uncle. It's good in some cases and very bad in others."

(*On stage:*)

FATHERS: So let's get right to the crux of it: You want to send me to the dustbin of history, to disenchant my power over you, to *kill* me.

(AND SONS): You're just like those old generals Marx, Weber, and

Freud, always ready to fight the last theory war. This is not about you and me: This is about a late modern condition where ambiguity and contingency, speed and surveillance, spectacle and simulation rule. The worry over theoretical heroes and heroic theories is touching but not very timely.[11]

FATHERS: But then what do we have to talk about?

(AND SONS): Not much.

(*Take two:*)

FATHERS: Let's start again. How do you explain the new interest in theory in IR?

(AND SONS): The easy answer? It's simply a generational anxiety triggered not by the end of history but by its acceleration. What once appeared transparent and predictable has taken on a strange new veneer, simultaneously superficial and opaque. As history conspires to reduce the international relations theorist to the intellectual status of armchair pundit, *decline denial* sets in. You can see it in the schizophrenic split of the traditionalist camp of IR in the United States, with the cynical neo-Machiavellians on one side, feeding on new perceptions of persecution while clinging to the reasonable belief that history will repeat. This of course allows them to recycle ideas and lecture notes one more time before retirement. On the other side, we find the hubristic neo-Hegelians, pumped up with a chauvinist pride that grows before the fall, who have unilaterally declared an end to history, leading some in their ranks to gloat while others wax nostalgic.

FATHERS: And where do you find yourself?

(AND SONS): Trying to think anew about new problems, in spite of and in opposition to the disciplinary conformity that stifles such efforts. But that conformity seems to be breaking up. I believe that the current proliferation of approaches that we are witnessing matches not just the depth and breadth of new problems but also the loss in a consensus on the best means to measure and map the new spaces of world politics.

FATHERS: But hasn't every generation of scholars viewed their era, their predicament, their theories as the most dangerous, the most turbulent, the most radical?

(AND SONS): I agree—and dissent. To paraphrase R.E.M. ...

FATHERS: What?

(AND SONS): My point precisely. Michael Stipe of R.E.M. sings that it is the end of the world—*as we know it*. What this means is that before we can know and, in the act of knowing, reconstruct a "new" world, we face the perpetual task of deconstructing "old" epistemologies: Otherwise, "endism" begets yet another cycle of mythical "originism." This move is fully evidenced in your writings as well as in the recent spate of preferred readings on the decline of U.S. and USSR hegemony. What began as an intellectual attempt to understand the rise and fall of great powers quickly deteriorated into the elevation and denigration of particular scholars and their political sponsors: in other words, a metonymic event, or intellectual simulacrum of decline denial. It all started off as a collegial, indeed, Ivy League event, with Gilpin from Princeton kicking off to Kennedy from Yale who was first tackled by Nye from Harvard. Then play was stopped when Fukuyama from State walked off the field with the ball, declaring an end to the game (and going free-agent to pick up a new million-dollar book contract).

FATHERS: So you see no progress, no hope for a general theory of IR, no better worlds?

(AND SONS): Not now, not when grand theory goes schizo. When the preferred readings of declining hegemonic powers split, distort, and weaken, we *should* expect some pretty bizarre symptoms in the field of IR. But over and against the background noise of dissent, a powerful message can still be heard. It echoes Hegel (but without the irony) when he states in *The Phenomenology of Spirit* that "Happy peoples have no history." Crudely templated to our own experience, this means now that we have won the Cold War (the only meaningful war), it is time—as it was immediately following the two other great conflicts of the twentieth century—for us to settle into a new political as well as epistemological isolationism. But I would argue from the above evidence that the victory celebrations have deafened the most superpowerful scholars to a host of new and urgent messages. In effect, they have unilaterally left the proverbial forest with the falling trees, where the majority of peoples of the world are unhappily making history and yet trying to make sense of all the noise.[12]

FATHERS: (*with increasing exasperation*): But where do *you* stand?

(AND SONS): I suppose somewhere in this constructed space of a false quiet. One can detect the traces of dissonance—generational, cultural, sexual—that run silent, run deep, and never quite break the surface tension of your theory, or for that matter, IR discourse in general. Perhaps they are little noticed or under-debated because they threaten to break the bounds of civil dialogue and further divide the field between those who hear noise and those who hear music, between those who say the party is over and those who say let's party, between those who see tradition as a safe harbor and those who see it as an anchor.

Scene 2
Mother Courage (and Her Children): Re-forming IR?

FATHERS (*cross-dressed as MOTHER COURAGE*): I think it's about time that we heard some female voices in IR—as long as they don't sound too shrill, or god forbid, too French.[13]

(AND SONS) (*keeping a wary eye out for [HER CHILDREN]*): I'm not sure that it matters what you think. An insurgent matrix of generational and gendered difference has already created pressure from below and outside the discipline. So why rehearse lines that have been better executed by others?[14]

(HER CHILDREN) (*arriving*): Like the threads, Mom. Care to check my papers before I enter this dialogue?

FATHERS (*dressed-down*): Always trying to provoke me, aren't you?

(HER CHILDREN): Well, I could force my way in, but that's more your style.

FATHERS: A cheap shot.

(HER CHILDREN): Is it? Have you ever looked up "force" in Web-
ster's? The first definition is "to make a person (or animal) do
something by force; compel." The second is, simply, "to rape (a
woman)." You've got to love those parentheses.

FATHERS: So what's your belabored point?

(HER CHILDREN): Very simple: In international relations, force
equals rape. You have nations violated, interfered with in a violent manner. The recurring "rape" of Poland, or the "rape" of
Czechoslovakia, are powerful, transhistorical analogues. In international relations (and dictionaries), women (like animals)
suffer a parenthetical rape: It happens at the edges of war and
colonial conquest and appears only at the fringes of a few classical narratives.[15]

(AND SONS): So boys are bad and girls are good?

(HER CHILDREN): Nice try, but as long as we're the dominant voice
in this act, reductio ad absurdum won't cut it. I'm not saying
that *all* violence is phallocentric, or that feminist IR should
confine itself to such a thesis. I'm just trying to open up for discussion what some in the field consider to be an inappropriate
motivation for scholarly research: righteous anger. And here I
refer not only to violence against women but the role of
phallocentric force against men as well. If you believe that the
civilizing march of progress has rendered this an archaic and
inappropriate topic for IR, than I suggest you take a look at a
video I brought along.

(*The videotape from a prime-time news program opens with a
long overhead shot of a Hungarian in freshly de-stalinized Ro-
mania being brutally beaten. A small group of men disperse after
the beating, except for one man who lingers and aims a final kick
at the supine Hungarian's testicles. The dead man doesn't move:
Satisfied, the live one moves on. It is a loop video.*)

MOTHER COURAGE: All fine and good, but your anger is just the
mirror image of male violence. Where will that get you?

(HER CHILDREN): Why should I listen to you? Your so-called courage is nothing more than a willingness to accept defeat on the
big issues while gaining the petty victories that allow you to

survive the Theory Wars. Your cynicism, your numbing of outrage, and your reduction of expectations—you are nothing but
a realist *poseur.*

MOTHER COURAGE: "You listen because you know I'm right. Your
rage has calmed down already. It was a short one and you'd
need a long one. But where would you find it?"[16]

(HER CHILDREN): There's plenty of injustice to go around.

MOTHER COURAGE: You think that a global anger will re-form a
global condition? Take it from an old camp follower: It's better
to feed the Theory Wars than to be its sacrificial fodder.

FATHERS (AND SONS): Speaking of food, where's the beef?

Scene 3
The Dog (and the Beef)

(SON) (*approaches the front of the cave*): Who are you?

DOG: Where's the beef?

(SON): What beef?

DOG (*barks but does not bite*): Grrrr.

(SON): There's more on the menu of life than beef. Have you tried
tofu?

DOG: Grrrrr.

(SON): Okay, Okay. What kind of beef? Chuck, flank, filet mignon?

DOG: Beef is beef.

(SON): Yes and no. In some cultures beef is used as a ritual sacrifice to the gods. And believe it or not, some people use it to signify something of substance, like, say, a research program.

*Suddenly a little old lady, Walter Mondale, and Ronald Reagan ap-
pear. She begins to hit Mondale over the head with an umbrella for
taking her beef patty. Reagan, having no beef, is grinning widely.
The DOG goes for the leg of the (SON), who grabs the burger from
Mondale and gives it to the DOG. The DOG lets go of the (SON)'s leg*

and disappears into the cave. The (SON) is left alone in front of the cave. A strange creature approaches.

(SON): Where's the beef?

Epilogue

I would like to end by returning to the theme that set the stage of Rosenau's dialogue: the impact of rapid change on IR. Rosenau deserves much credit: Confronting a strange new world, SAR does not leave the forest for the manicured suburbs of IR. He witnesses the rapidity of change and interprets the turbulence of international relations as intellectual imperatives for opening up the discipline to questions of cultural difference, generational identity, and critical approaches. But I think SAR might be making a possibly fatal error: He seems to be running to catch up to events that are in fact bearing down on him at very high speed.

Let me explain this point with a few outtakes from the remarkable events in Eastern and Central Europe. First, there is the speech by President Vaclav Havel of Czechoslovakia to the joint session of the Congress in February 1990, widely (but not very deeply) covered in the media. His opening remarks highlighted the acceleration of history: "The human face of the world is changing so rapidly that none of the familiar political speedometers are adequate. We playwrights, who have to cram a whole human life or an entire historical era into a two-hour play, can scarcely understand this rapidity ourselves."[17] Curiously, the *New York Times* excerpted the above remarks in the following day's paper but expurgated Havel's completion of the thought: "And if it gives us trouble think of the trouble it must give to political scientists who spend their whole life studying the realm of the probable and have even less experience with the realm of the improbable than the playwrights."[18]

The easy criticism, one that does not break the rationalist (or alliterative) constraints of Rosenau's entitlement, is that superpower scholars are too *slow*: They/we have lost the alacrity and celerity to keep up with events. This observation echoes Carr's concern that historians are failing to evolve in synchronicity with structural changes in world politics. But left out of the equation is an important new force in IR: the acceleration of mass by information.

A second outtake: the circle of Peter Jennings quoting playwright (not yet President) Vaclav Havel who was quoting the scholar-journalist Timothy Garton Ash: "In Poland it took ten years, in Hungary ten months, in East Germany ten weeks; perhaps in Czechoslovakia it will take ten days."[19]

Events in the Soviet Union, Eastern Europe, and Central Europe give eloquent testimony to the pace, improvisation, and intertextuality of change. But the lesson I have drawn from these events clearly exceeds Carr's or Rosenau's prescriptions for understanding rapid change. The real-time representation and transmission of global change are such that running to keep up with events is no longer sufficient. International relations is passing, I believe, from what could be called a classical *Heraclitian dilemma* to a postmodern *Doppler conundrum*. In effect, there is a new game of chicken being played out in IR between the onrushing event and the sometimes recoiling, sometimes advancing observer, who becomes unsure of the source and direction of change: Is it varying according to its relative velocity to the observer? Is it being warped by the mediation of transmission? Is it, in short, objectively knowable, before it is upon or beyond us? Global change is now witnessed as closely and as similarly as the passing of a train is first experienced, and we seem to be simultaneously repelled from and attracted to the waxing and warping of a new power that might just leap the rails.

Paul Virilio, whose work has gone largely unnoticed in IR, has given serious consideration to the political effects of excessive or insufficient speed in our systems of weapons, communications, and decisionmaking.[20] Virilio believes a revolution has taken place in the regulation of speed: "Space is no longer in geography—it's in electronics. Unity is in the terminals. It's in the instantaneous time of command posts, multi-national headquarters, control towers, etc. ... There is a movement from geo- to chronopolitics: the distribution of territory becomes the distribution of time. The distribution of territory is outmoded, minimal."[21] But where does this leave the superpower scholar? Out of breath or full of bluster? Extraterritorial and patriotic? Bewildered yet cynical? Passive or active?

A third outtake: better to bank on a dated metanarrative than risk a new adventure in story-telling: "But Mr. Norris said when it comes to ideas for screenplays, he's staying away from the fast-moving events in Eastern Europe."[22]

Or, finally, a fourth outtake: from Adam Michnik, a powerful rebuttal and lesson from the Solidarity leader who found the events in Eastern Europe extraordinary and exceptionalist: "A striking characteristic of the totalitarian system is its peculiar coupling of human demoralization and mass depoliticizing. Consequently, battling this system requires a conscious appeal to morality and an inevitable involvement in politics. This is how the singular anti-political political movement emerged in Central and Eastern Europe."[23]

My last words to Rosenau? It is in the very *de-scription* of IR that we might write an antidiplomatic diplomatic dialogue for its future.

ACT V

"Bringing It All Back Home, Again"[1]

Jean Bethke Elshtain

Senior American Feminist Scholar (SAFS), Skeptical Intelligent Concerned Citizen (SICC), and their compatriots, all somewhat alienated attendees at the annual meeting of the International Studies Association, are seated at a bar. It is the end of a long day; they have attended several panels and informal "kitchen debates." At one of these, they overheard a heated, acerbic exchange between SAR and JUSOFS. They are now tired, bored, or simply muddled about how to respond.

SAFS and SICC attended undergraduate school together in the 1960s. SAFS opted for an academic career as a feminist political theorist. SICC bounced around as an activist and sometime journalist, winding up as a political columnist, not a particularly famous one but a respected observer of the political scene. When SICC really wants to wound SAFS, he accuses her of starting out to "do good" and then winding up "doing well." SAFS in turn accuses SICC of professional jealousy and nostalgic anti-institutionalism. In other words, these two are very good friends.

SAFS: Sometimes I feel jaded—maybe just old—you know, the sort of feeling that gets expressed in cliched ways: "There's nothing new under the sun," or "The more things change, the more they stay the same," or "I've heard all this before." That old déjà vu. More accurately, it might be, "I don't even want to hear this once."

(Her compatriots stare into their drinks and nod sympathetically.

97

No one pipes up to disagree, but then again, there's no clarion cry of approval either. There is a prolonged moment of silence.)

SICC: Say more, what's brought on this curiously dyspeptic mood? The bad nachos or the impenetrable papers and interminable squabbles or all or none of the above?

(*At this point the rest of the company defects. They were present at an animated verbal duel between SAFS and SICC just the night before and have no desire to repeat the experience.*)

SAFS: Now who's dyspeptic? I was just reflecting a mood. You seem to be dispensing a judgment—a judgment based on attendance at your first ISA, I believe.

SICC: And last! No heat. No light. Just academic turf wars so far as I can tell. Oh, sure, there are critics and rebels running around—self-described—but I must tell you that to put together "academic" and "rebel" is to generate a risible oxymoron.

SAFS: Okay. I can see it coming. Unreconstructed 1960s *Schadenfreude*. Quasi-contemptuous musings about how miserable academics are, especially those who somehow sold out and should be out in the world being revolutionaries, god knows how, but somehow, rather than pronouncing blessings and anathemas from their safe perch in the ivy-covered ...

SICC: Hold on SAFS. You were always too quick on the trigger. You know what I'm talking about. You're being purposely obtuse. I mean most academic rebellion comes down to turf wars. Sure, those involved may start out from some lofty plane, but then it all turns into strategy and "who is the enemy, who the ally" sort of stuff and who can get the most bucks for the bang (or the whimper) from which big granting agency and who got what sort of offer and who got screwed (pardon the French) by whom when it was tenure or promotion time and ...

SAFS: Hold on, Roy Rogers. Good lord. I suppose political journalism is one sustained friendly hand-holding session between Mahatma Gandhi and Mother Teresa.

SICC: Well, you tell me, then. What the hell good is international relations as an academic enterprise where real politics is concerned? I mean, maybe that guy JUSOFS has a point—high academic IR is "hooked into the interstate system," you know, the academic arm of the powers-that-be. Why not? Think of Voltaire, that great defender of free thought, trekking off to be a one-man think tank for Frederick the Great of Prussia—not exactly a constitutional democrat. Some of SUKA's biting asides about the well-fed, privileged, and hegemonic American IR scholar and his—or her for that matter—why should we expect the women to be any different when they become establishment?—world of power ploys and plays in the groves of academe seem to me well placed. And TSITSI's concerns about the dangers inherent in Western feminism's defining what is going on—a danger WESTFEM clearly recognized in that discussion we overheard—are also on the mark. As for the Barthe and Baudrillard stuff that postmodern guy was talking about—what the hell is that? What does that have to do with anything? If this is rebellion, it is rebellion of a pretty rarefied sort if nobody can figure out what the point is. I mean, the postmoderns think everybody else belongs in a museum. But maybe they belong in a cineplex, you know, one of those ultramodern entertainment complexes where you're visually overstimulated at every point and ... well, let me just say that I didn't find much guidance in this whole affair.

SAFS: So that's it. You attend ISA thinking it's church and you're going to hear a sermon and get your marching orders and go out and do good in the world. Grow up! Guidance? These are not counseling sessions. I don't know where to start with your bewildered vehemence. Maybe with this point for now, and then I, for one, will need another glass of white wine, but no more of those crummy, soggy nachos. And the point is this, just to defend at least one dimension of the postmodern plaint as I understand it. The most forceful argument coming from such scholars is that much of the previous "guidance" proffered by the theorists and systematizers and modelers was folly—not only wrong but downright dangerous because such efforts, historic and contemporary, presumed we had or could have control over events that in fact we do not have. Gone is the world of the "metanarrative"—where a strong, overarching story of the

March of Progress or some such could run roughshod over particular, concrete realities and help us to forget, for example, the mounds of bodies on which the nation-state rests and ...

SICC: Why do we need the postmoderns to tell us that? That was Camus's argument against the "Socialism of the Gallows," wasn't it? Against Sartre and all that metatheorizing that theorizes the life out of things and can even delude itself into justifying the gulags in the name of some future good.[2]

SAFS: Well, of course. You and I have always agreed about Camus. It's the only reason I keep talking to you—that and the fact that you can remember the titles of Bob Dylan songs when I come up with bits of lyric but don't know which song they belong to.

SICC: Haven't you just wiped out your defense of the attack against metanarrative?

SAFS: No, I don't think so. Every epoch generates its own voices, its own point and counterpoint. And there is much lively counterpoint in these challenges, whether they offer you direct political guidance or not.

SICC: I still don't get it, really. I know I'm inviting you to mount the soapbox, but flesh this out and tell me, if you would, what feminism has to do with it. Isn't feminism a strong metanarrative? Doesn't it promise some new and better world if we get rid of bad old states or bad old men or bad old violence and all that?

SAFS: Come on, you can do better than that. Of course, there are feminisms that push for hegemony, some all-encompassing narrative, theory, or model—I call them "narratives of closure" because they leave no room for ambiguity; instead, they aspire to hard and fast truths on the grand scale and eliminate complexity, irony, and paradox as corrosive of totalized ideological commitment. Now, let me see if I can remember—I once enumerated the markers of a narrative of closure and, as far as I'm concerned, if the shoe fits, wear it. I meant to criticize any and all such theories, whether feminist, nonfeminist, antifeminist, political economy, rational choice, realist, neorealist—I don't care.

sicc: All right. So we know you like being feisty. Give me the criteria, will you? That is, if you can remember them.

safs: Okay. This is what you should not do or seek or create. It is my theoretical cautionary tale to all scholars everywhere. What characterizes a narrative (theory, model) of closure is one or more of the following—and, by the way, you can have "strong" or "weak" closure, depending on how many categories fit—(1) a search for some "original position" from which history has proceeded, with this beginning determining its forward movement; (2) a clearly identified, universally construed object of critique (for example, patriarchal culture, capitalist society, or world communism) that gives the political agenda supported by the narrative its form and meaning; (3) an explicit or implied universal subject, one generic human type; (4) a dehistoricizing sweep that deflects from cultural and political particularity in a search for the key to all ways of life, every political act, and so on; (5) a predetermined end point, whether in the creation of a benign new and better "sex gender system" that would eliminate violence altogether, or a classless Communist utopia, or a world of freely cooperating free-market societies— you know, the coming of the kingdom on this earth; (6) finally, an Archimedean point that offers the analyst claims of epistemological privilege. Whew! That was exhausting if not exhaustive.[3]

sicc: Okay. That just about does it. You have now eliminated the possibility for any coherent theory any place any time. I never took you for a—what should I call it?—a subjectivist or anarchist or whatever this comes to.

safs: If you were as hyperbolic in print as you are in conversation you could do your own TV talk show. There is nothing, I repeat—nothing—in what I just negated, so to speak, that precludes coherence, affirmation, or argument. Indeed, I would insist that to cease and desist from grand narratives of closure, to move instead toward perspectives and positions that, more modestly and surefootedly, give us insight, even insistencies robustly defended and drawing upon strong but various evidence—I'm not anti-empirical—is by far the better way to go as scholars and citizens. Alan Ryan, in a review essay in the *Times Literary Supplement,* commented along these lines: "It is ... absurd to demand what the social sciences can't deliver. They can at best illuminate what *has* happened, not predict what will; describe the politician's opportunities, not tell him how to act."[4]

SICC: Remember, I'm the amateur here. The concerned citizen. What big issues—you know, pervasive concerns—have been, how shall I put it, distorted, let's say, by being argued in and through one of those "narratives of closure" you indict. And what's the alternative? I need ...

SAFS: Guidance again?

(*Having had four beers, SICC moves to one of his two characteristic modes—"the monosyllabic"—the other being "the voluble."*)

SICC: So?

SAFS: All right. Let's just take violence, if you want a big issue. And then, for good measure, we'll take peace. That ought to be grand and booming enough for you. I'm thinking of Hannah Arendt's indictment of a teleology of violence.[5] Arendt exposes our acceptance of politics as war by other means. Her reference point is Western politics and political thought, but I doubt she would exempt any tradition from the indictment; certainly the Islamic world has not been "pacifist" in its dominant modes of expression, as but one example. Moreover, she asks what historic transformations and discursive practices made possible "a nigh-consensus among political theorists from Left to Right ... that violence is nothing more than the most flagrant manifestation of power?" The violence she has in mind, by the way, is that of groups or collectives, not an individual's outrage culminating in a single violent act. And her answer—typically Arendtian—is multiple: She cites teleological constructions of historic inevitability—progress, let's say; theories of absolute power as dominion tied to the emergence of the nation-state; command obedience conceptions of law, theologically justified in some instances; the infusion of biologism into political discourse; and the notion (uplifted by Futurists, at one point, as

well as by Sorelians and Sartrians) that destruction and violence can be life-promoting forces through which men purge
the old and the rotten. All these "time-honored opinions have
become dangerous." Locked into a self-confirming way of
thinking, embracing "progress" as a standard of evaluation, we
manage to convince ourselves that good will comes out of terrible things; that somehow, in history, the end does justify the
means. Arendt is especially critical of the "great trust in the dia-
lectical power of negation that soothes its adherents into be-
lieving that evil is but a temporary manifestation of a still human good." Now Arendt makes this exposé because she wants
to open up space for politics, for what she calls "political being," and move away from a teleology of violence and the notion that history is a train, so to speak, with a fixed destination.
Following this approach is one way, perhaps the only way,
given the fragility and uncertainty of human lives, that we can
resist reducing politics to domination. Consequently, she offers
up a plenary jolt to our reigning political metaphors and categories—such as state of nature, sovereignty, statism, bureau-
cratization, contractualism, nationalistic triumphalism, and
ideological triumphalism of any kind—including utopian fantasies of perfect worlds, or especially such fantasies.

SICC: Well, you know I'm a sucker for that sort of argument; so I'm
prepared to be seduced by it and hoist another beer and con-
gratulate us both on being so wise. But, come on, SAFS, why
isn't this nostalgic in its own way—a world without domination
and the like? Doesn't Arendt get a little goody-goody here?

SAFS: I don't think so. To be sure, her arguments are elusive at
points. But she insists one cannot foreordain the outcome of a
genuine political moment—a moment when people act in
common together. There are ethical limits to such action implicit in her indictment of violence, it seems to me.

SICC: What does she say about international issues? We are, after
all, in the heart of the beast at ISA, are we not—with people
who concentrate on what goes on between states and other international "actors" (as I've learned to say).

SAFS: Well, I'm sorry you asked, really. She throws in the towel a bit

on that one and just opts for the view that warfare is with us because no substitute for this final arbiter in international affairs
has yet appeared on the political scene. Was not Hobbes right
when he said: "Covenants, without the sword, are but words"?[6]
Arendt isn't flat-out wrong on this issue, but she never bothers
to argue the point out the way, say, Kenneth Waltz does in *Man,
the State and War.*[7] She defines power as that which happens
when people act together toward certain ends that they have
debated, and violence as the way authentic power/politics gets
destroyed. But I just don't get how she squares her sharp distinction between power and violence with her Hobbesian
leap—you know, Hobbes's bleak view that all humankind is
dominated by a "restless striving for power after power that
ceaseth only in death."

SICC: You're probably demanding more from Arendt than you
should. You sound personally disappointed.

SAFS: So?

SICC: Let me just say that attacking violence is pretty safe, isn't it?
Nobody actually endorses it, not even those guys running
around who say it is inevitable, the coin of the international
realm, so to speak.

SAFS: Now I've gotcha. To say something is "inevitable" is to hook
oneself into the teleology Arendt indicts, and that amounts to a
tacit endorsement.

SICC: Listen, I've known you too long to go along with this line you
seem to be pushing. Weren't you the one always raining on the
peace parades even when you went marching? You said most of
the folks were naive and utopian and there couldn't be a world
without violence and …

SAFS: There's no inconsistency here. I'm prepared to attack
Peace—in caps, as a historic teleology—as well. Want to hear
how this goes?

SICC: Well, I don't guess I have much choice. And I don't think I'm
up to another panel on rent-seeking states. What the hell is that
anyway? The state as a landlord? Are there rent-controlled
zones? Who collects? I mean …

SAFS: You don't want to know, believe me. It has to do with a big econometric move on the part of some analysts—apolitical and reductive, if you ask me. But I don't want to talk about that. I want to talk about the Problem with Peace. So, it goes like this: The problem is that Peace is an ontologically suspicious concept.[8] By that I mean that peace emerged as the absolute opposition to a state of war and disorder. Peace never appears without war framing the discussion. Better put, peace is inside, not outside, a frame with war—especially in the most absolute and utopian expressions of its desirability and realizability. War is threatening disorder; peace is healing order. As you know, there are some feminists who argue that war comes down to male aggressivity and that it can be countered by a feminism that sees power in an ostensibly "healthy form"—in other words, by a "holistic understanding" of power that leads to a cooperative and nurturing harmonious existence. This, then, is an inversion that winds up requiring that which is opposed—an absolutized vision of war and conflict.

SICC: Okay, I get the conceptual picture. But suppose someone comes back at you and says that all you're left with, if you give up on—what would you call it?—the great and glorious hope, the metanarrative of Peace—is a world of half-measures and various pacts with various devils and the like? Would this be what a "realist" would say? Except that the realist wouldn't put it so caustically, presumably, because he—and I guess we usually think of realists as "hes," despite all sorts of historic evidence that women can think and act in Hobbesian sorts of ways. At least you've convinced me of this much so I don't look to women as the collective saviors of humankind anymore.

SAFS: Thanks for relieving me of the burden of gender!

SICC: Ah, come on. You agree with me on this. But where does that leave you or anyone else who gives up on the Big Picture of war versus peace?

SAFS: I've proposed a few times the following thought experiment: Suppose the "war system," shorthand for sovereign states in conflict with one another, in a permanent agon, were eliminated. What forms of conflict would occur? What alternative conceptualizations of struggle do we imagine?[9]

SICC: What's the answer?

SAFS: The answer is complicated, obviously, and I'm going to resist the temptation to answer you directly, despite your clamor
about "guidance" a while back, because I want to talk a little
more epistemology talk.

SICC: Is that what this has been?

SAFS: Well, not exclusively. There's been ontological talk as well,
and ...

SICC: Never mind this. More along these lines and I will seek out
the rent-seekers!

SAFS: Listen, be patient with just this much, okay? What I want to
insist on here is that, even if over-ambitious systematization
were out, the alternative would not be a collapse into empathy—you know, some thoroughgoing identification with "op-
pressed people everywhere," not only or simply because this
attitude easily becomes rather patronizing but because it does
not permit the necessary critical distance and analytic acuity.
We can't settle problems of knowledge and truth here tonight.

SICC (*sotto voce*): Thank you, lord.

SAFS (*pretending not to hear*): But we can, minimally, insist that
there may not be a neutral, independent viewpoint from which
to view our culture or other cultures. This premise makes ever
more exigent, not less, the need for critical perspicuity and
strong argument that invites counterargument and leads, I
would hope, to a robust rather than an anemic dialogue. In
other words, we can insist both that forms of life are not, as the
philosophers say, "incorrigible"—that just means that everything can be criticized rather than simply "empathized with"—
and that there *is* some "truth" to the matter—truth with a small
"t," not a large one. This approach is easier to work when one is
dealing with persons and their self-understandings; harder, but
not impossible, when it comes to cultures. Charles Taylor talks
about an epistemology of interpretation that turns on "perspic-
uous contrasts"—understanding some other society means
understanding one's own better as well, and neither is exempt

from criticism.[10] There are no pure villains, no pure victims. No harmonious sanctuaries, and very few absolute hells. Maybe I'm leaping rather precipitously from epistemology to worldview, but I think you get the picture. We have to have a way of accounting for difference and variation—not simply re-mark on it or "leave space" for it. And by "accounting for," I don't mean analysis interminable; I mean doing the best one can following always the rule that there is no "key," no set of sanitized assumptions and all-purpose theorems.

SICC (*beginning to waver, eyelids at half-mast, and yawning dra-matically*): All right. I can see all of this through a glass darkly at the moment but, SAFS, my friend, where is the politics, or what of the politics? We have all these new nations popping up, and nobody knows what's to become of nuclear warheads and trig-ger devices. We have armies running around without a home. Navies in dry dock in Russia going nuts from boredom and get-ting restless from lack of pay. The Middle East remains a tinder-box. Western Europe is probably permanently settled down. The U.S. is the one remaining superpower. For all the talk about declining American hegemony—and on some economic level that might be true—politically and militarily and even culturally the U.S. is king of the mountain, loved and hated as are all kings, and we're sitting at a meeting where scholars are supposed to be sorting all this out despite the fact that, to my knowledge, nobody foresaw 1989 and all the breathtaking stuff since and ...

SAFS: You can't go to sleep on me now. Let me have a go at some of this. I'll keep it crisp, pithy, violently abrupt. The major political force in the world today is nationalism. The twenty-first cen-tury—call this a prophecy uttered in a moment of reckless dis-cursive abandon—will be the century of nations and religion, all the things certain legalists and internationalists and Whigs and rationalists thought would go away, wither, and die a well-deserved death. Every successful revolution since 1945, as Ben-edict Anderson has pointed out, has been defined in national terms. The end of nationalism is "not remotely in sight." This is even truer today than when Anderson wrote his book *Imagined Communities* in 1983.[11] Anderson argues that nationalism invents nations where they do not exist. For example, many have argued that the experience of dispossession and occupation has in fact *created* Palestinian nationalism and that it is a force that must now be reckoned with. And the way that reckoning tends to take place is through the construction of a state. Unsurprisingly, Palestinian women support the struggle for statehood. There is no doubt some irony in this, considering the fact that women share the burdens, the strife, and the national identity but are unlikely to share, in the way the liberal West understands it, official state power in the aftermath. But leave that aside for the moment. My point for now is that national identity is pervasive—not total, not uncritical—at least one hopes the skeptical moment is preserved, though that hope may be utopian on some grand scale—and that states as the "containers" for national identity are not only not disappearing, they are busting out all over, clamoring for recognition, for that may mean, quite literally, the difference between life and death.[12] States aren't the only "actors," of course, but I'd be prepared to argue, or at least defend the possibility, that some forms of the state represent the most realistic and realizable hope for a more decent, if not perfect, world. I have in mind—and this will sound awfully dull I'm sure—the liberal, constitutional state, a more social, less litigious, less individualistic liberalism than the contractarian view that dominates more and more in the United States. In other words, small wonder a bounded entity usually called a nation-state is sought by the powerless, who are often stymied by the powerful—imperialists, colonizers, and the like. A state affords at least some political power to the nonprivileged. Of course, it usually goes on to constitute its own forms of internal privilege, and that is a problem, no doubt, but ...

sicc: I thought this was supposed to be a dramatically self-limiting exercise on your part but, as usual, you have become more rather than less voluble. I think it may be time to call it a night. I have to head across town. A working man, excuse me, person, can't afford the high rent at an upscale hotel like this ...

(At this apparent denouement, the bar, nearly deserted, begins to grow befogged. A chill blast swishes past. SICC and SAFS experi-

ence a simultaneous frisson. What to their wondering eyes should appear but a small whirlwind as the fog concentrates. They are either in a Michael Jackson video or something even more strange is happening. The dense swirl begins to dissipate, and there before them, an apparition, pale and glowing eerily, stands as if at attention, enshrouded in a floor-length black cape. "[D]istill'd almost to jelly with the act of fear," they sit agape and the apparition, taking one step toward their table, speaks, sounding rather like John Gielgud as the ghost of Hamlet's father.)

APPARITION: I am GORP, the Ghost of Realism Past. I haven't come to "dialogue." That's not my style. But, then, you probably already know that. I am merely curious and a bit restless tonight. You know, these ISA meetings are a real trial to my spirit, a torment, if you will. But I thought you might be friendly company. Did I not hear someone mention "a restless striving after power that ceaseth only in death" a few moments ago? That was music to my ears.

(SICC and SAFS engage in a simultaneous expulsion, a gasp, if you will.)

GORP: Just kidding.

(SAFS and SICC are stunned into uncharacteristic silence.)

GORP: Has neither of you anything to say? I am a perturbed spirit, not only because of what I have been hearing, or not hearing, but because this is not my usual milieu. It also takes quite a bit of effort to make myself manifest.

SAFS *(having rediscovered her tongue)*: GORP, that's pretty hard to believe. You may not appear like this too often, but you are surely "manifest" all over the place. Hasn't realism won the discursive war against those labeled "idealists," who are readily dismissed as softheaded? Think about it. Don't most international relations scholars accept some variant on the theme that state sovereignty is the motor that moves the international system, that struggle is endemic to that system, and that force is the court of last resort? And there are all sorts of ways to "prove" these notions, from Thucydides to fancy models that assume at base, with Hobbes, that human beings are entities driven by appetite and aversion and ...

GORP: Please, forgive me, but I'm sure I wouldn't be feeling so bereft if this meeting reflected my views accurately. Also, I must tell you, SAFS, that you've been sounding rather like a friendly interlocutor in your exchanges with SICC. And this may surprise you, but I don't consider my old friend Tom Hobbes a "realist" at all. I never really went for that "state of nature" business. Oh, human beings can be nasty all right, and it is not even remotely in the cards that a conflict-free human condition is in store. But Tom, well, you know, he was in love with geometry and wanted to put everything on what he considered a scientific basis—compressed theorems and the like. His first published work was a translation of Thucydides, you know, and what he drew from Thucydides—someone I don't know personally, by the way, although he seems always to be lurking somewhere in the netherworld—was the view that history can teach us how to conduct ourselves. Well and good. But then he went too far with method, became an enthusiast about the notion that everything is caused by motion, and went on from that to the view that one could get sure and certain results. In human affairs, of all things!

SICC: I think I'm hearing things. I mean, I can't believe I'm hearing these things.

GORP: My friend, why not?

SICC: Well, isn't it the case that Thucydides and Machiavelli and Hobbes all belong in one tradition and this tradition has been more and more refined, if that's the word for it, and that now we have these models based on the assumptions embedded in the history of realism and ...

SAFS: SICC, I don't think contemporary "scientized" so-called realism is realistic at all!

GORP: SAFS is right. This is why I am a morose spirit. The problem, by the way, is not a problem with "abstraction," as some who urge more empathic or connected, as they call it, ways of thinking will tell you. One can't think in any way at all without abstractions. The problem is bizarre idealizations or ...

SAFS: I call it "abstractedness," a way of thinking that abstracts from history and the particularity of cultures and languages and anything like real political exigencies.

GORP (*beginning to take on a less ghostly aura, but never moving from his position*): Exactly. I wish I could join you for a drink but, well, you understand the problem (*sighs*). Let me proceed before I retreat into the world from whence I came. There are some young scholars who give me comfort. I heard their presentations. These scholars are challenging what has been done with Thucydides, for example, arguing that the generalizations Thucydides offered should not be taken as causal laws of politics but instead correspond to what some of your philosophers call "rule-governed behavior." To understand the elusive Thucydides, one must unravel the complex rhetorical universe and culture of argument he created.[13] No way did Thucydides offer up what some of your critical theorists and—what are they called?—postmoderns criticize, rightly, as "unitary givens." In fact, his story is a tragedy, and one of the reasons I am always a spirit of rather disconsolate visage is that history is tragic, is it not?

SICC: Ironic anyway.

SAFS: GORP, this is interesting. It seems to me, given what you've just said, that you would go along with what Joan Wallach Scott, a feminist historian, argued not long ago. She said: "Contests about meaning involve the introduction of new oppositions, the reversal of hierarchies, the attempt to expose repressed terms, to challenge the natural status of seemingly dichotomous pairs, and to expose their interdependence and their internal instability."[14]

GORP: Did I say something like that?

SICC (*chiming in before SAFS can respond*): SAFS, isn't this process of going back over classical texts what some feminist critics call "trying to defeat the master with his own weapons," hence futile from a feminist perspective?

SAFS: This issue is contested in feminism just as feminism itself is an essentially contested concept, if you will. But, remember, I am a political theorist, and I live with and work with these texts.

Also, we always "stand on the shoulders of giants," as St. Bernard of Clairvoux argued. Some of these giants are male, some female. In political theory, there are far more male giants for reasons much discussed, but this tradition is not of a piece. Jane Jaquette, in a long discussion of Machiavelli, argued that he wasn't the hard-core "scientific theorist" some have made him out to be—that he invented dialogue, deployed mythical modes of understanding, and was attuned to "contradiction, association, metaphor, and multiple, often antithetical points of view." Hence, Machiavelli offers up an "effective alternative to positivism," and I think one of the reasons GORP is so sad is that realism got captured by positivists, modelers, and those searching for causal covering laws and the like and lost its historic richness and its tragic or ironic sensibility. Jaquette, by the way, urges feminists to consider Machiavelli's approach as instructive; he illustrates the world of phronesis or "practical reason" in contrast to abstracted and universally categorical ways of thinking.[15] Mind you, I'm still not a Machiavellian, but this is worth considering.

GORP: A delightful fellow, Nicky, quite cunning.

SAFS: Yes, the cunning I can imagine in several senses of the word.

GORP: This is getting much too nice. Really. I fret about this apparent agreement. Suppose I insisted that sovereignty—final authority within a political region—and the sovereignty of instrumental reason—must reign supreme and that if they do not, all is folly.

SAFS: I would say you had lost your sense of irony—and historic acumen, for that matter. I believe we are obliged to criticize uncritical assumptions about sovereignty and pose it as a problem.

SICC: But you were defending the state just a few minutes ago, weren't you? Or was that a delusion I had before the apparition appeared?

SAFS: Yes, I was defending the notion of bounded political entities, but that doesn't mean they have to be sovereign in the classical sense—with absolute power and the authority to lay down the law in a unitary way and to permit no resort beyond the sovereign or sovereign state and all that. You know, I'm an antistatist deep down in my bones. But I'm also a realist and not a ghost, if you will forgive me, GORP. Can't the notion of a homeland and of sovereignty as a limited concept, rather like the franchise, come to prevail? Just like the vote, sovereignty offers political standing and in fact enables us to defend the integrity of particular ways of life—not their inviolability but their integrity. This notion seems to me far more compatible with feminism than seeking to leapfrog over cultures and their creation of political entities of a bounded sort in favor of some watery universalism. Look, you can't have it both ways. You can't condemn universal categories, concepts, and views of human beings and the like and then go on to trash the concepts and institutional arrangements necessary to protect particular identities. In a way, the desovereignizing (sorry, awkward word) of political entities—even as one continues to respect the notion of political independence, an independence that recognizes and even promotes forms of interdependence—seems to be not only absolutely necessary but essential to a robust feminist politics.[16]

SICC: Time out, time out! What is happening here? States but no sovereignty, or maybe sovereignty but it gets called independence or …

GORP: I'm a bit confused myself, perhaps because I am beginning to dematerialize. I suggest you be brief if you expect me to hear what you have to say.

SAFS: Must you really go? It would be great if you showed up for the panel on "Neorealism and Its Critics" tomorrow. I think Robert Keohane would get a big kick out of your presence—you could be a discussant, a mystery discussant appearing suddenly from, well, out of nowhere. Never mind. What I want to say before you swirl out of here is that your old notion of sovereignty, even with the ironic elements you built in, was too automatic, in a sense, in its demand for blood-sacrifice. This "will-to-sacrifice," as I call it, got encoded into modern identities, male and female, with the triumph of the modern nation-state. Now, it has ancient roots, of course. But I want to suggest moving to a postsovereign politics, a politics that shifts the focus of political loyalty and identity from sacrifice to responsibility. In other words, to a politics where the claims of sovereignty are chastened, the demands lowered and challenged, and the will-to-sacrifice supplanted by a more skeptical, critical sense of political identity. This is what many feminists are talking about, or at least a few are talking about it and more will be, I'm sure, as we enter the next century. This politics is open to all sorts of pressures—both "foreign" and "domestic." I'm thinking about the Mothers of the Plaza de Mayo—the Mothers of the Disap-peared—in Argentina, for example, who challenged the claims of a terroristic state apparatus, absolutist in its sovereign triumphalism, with an ethical politics grounded in human rights. Human rights now is an international discourse, and en-gaging in that discourse is sometimes the only way human be-ings have to fight state terror or political terror. But when they do so they are "not alone," so to speak, because an entire inter-national movement, which is institutionalized and becoming more and more effective, links up with them. The idea of the nation can, I think, be "deeply nonaggressive"; a plea for "cul-tural self-determination" can not only be comfortable with the possibility of coexistence but even insistent upon it. The "plu-rality of cultures is irreducible," and that plurality is best recog-nized in and through institutions that create and protect inde-pendence. "Once pluralism of ways of life is accepted, and there can be mutual esteem between different, uncombinable outlooks, it is difficult to suppose that all this can be flattened-out—*gleichgeschaltet*—by some huge, crushing jackboot."[17] And such entities offer political space within which questions of gender and other forms of inequality can be debated. Until people have some guarantee of communal or community safety and order, however, these issues will be on the back burner. That is just the way of it—all the evidence points in this direction.

GORP: I really must be disappearing. I feel a bit less morose, but fi-nally, you know, I am a hopeful spirit. The human comedy con-tinues!

(GORP *departs less grandly than he arrived—a poof, the air alive with particulates, then nothing.*)

SICC: What was in these drinks? Where are we? Who did you hire to put on that show? I'm outta here.

SAFS: But tell me what you think.

SICC: Think, at this hour? I'm barely breathing. I'm not thinking. I'm going home, and I'll read this one-page lecture, "On Home" by Vaclav Havel, as my final activity of the day or early morning, whatever it is. Will that suit you?

SAFS: Sure, he's the most eloquent spokesman for this new politics of limits I've been talking about. And he's desperately trying to hold the line against fanatics of all sorts, right and left, in the new, now divided, Czech and Slovak republics. A Camusian character, a mensch. Drinks are on me, SICC; otherwise you'll be proclaiming your shattered financial status over the next two days. If I pay, you're mum on money, deal?

SICC: Yeah, okay, I'll take the pledge. But you know it's under duress and counts for zilch.

SAFS: Who was that cloaked man, or actor, or entity, anyhow?

(*The scene shifts to SICC's bedroom. He stumbles into bed and stares at the photocopy of Havel's honorary degree speech at Lehigh University on October 26, 1991, "On Home," for a few moments. But he can't really focus. The paper slides from his fingers and slips to the floor. He doesn't awaken as GORP rematerializes with the usual fanfare, having got his second wind. GORP picks up the sheet and reads:*)

My home is the house I live in, the village or town where I was born or where I spend most of my time. My home is my family, the world of my friends, the social and intellectual milieu in which I live, my profession, my company, my work place. My home, obviously, is also the country I live in, the language I speak, and the intellectual and spiritual climate of my country expressed in the language spoken there. The Czech language, the Czech way of perceiving the world, Czech historical experience, the Czech modes of courage and cowardice, Czech humor—all of these are inseparable from that circle of my home. My home is therefore my Czechness, my nationality, and I see no reason at all why I shouldn't embrace it, since it is as essential a part of me as, for instance, my masculinity, another aspect of my home. My home, of course, is not only my

Czechness, it is also my Czechoslovakness, which means my citizenship. Ultimately, my home is Europe and my Europeanness and—finally—it is this planet and its present civilization and, understandably, the whole world. ... I think that every circle, every aspect of the human home, has to be given its due. ... I am in favor of a political system based on the citizen, and recognizing all his fundamental civil and human rights in their universal validity, and equally applied: that is, no member of a single race, a single nation, a single sex, or a single religion may be endowed with basic rights that are any different from anyone else's. In other words, I am in favor of what is called a civic society. ... To establish a state on any other principle than the civic principle ... means making one aspect of our home superior to all the others, and thus reduces us as people. ... The sovereignty of the community, the region, the nation, the state—any higher sovereignty, in fact—makes sense only if it is derived from the one genuine sovereignty, that is, from human sovereignty, which finds its political expression in civic sovereignty.[18]

(*Pause.*)

GORP: A little too nice, I think, but not bad, not bad at all.

(*GORP slips the single sheet under his cape and particularizes himself into noncorporeality. In the meantime, back at the conference hotel, SAFS is debating whether to incorporate the encounter with GORP into her paper for a panel on "Gender and IR: What Difference Does Difference Make?" She decides against it.*)

SAFS: GORP would be taken for a trope, not a trump. Besides, apparitions are not really in these days, and they were pretty scary centuries ago. Didn't Horatio caution Hamlet against following the ghost, saying it "might deprive your sovereignty of reason/ And draw you into madness"? (*SAFS chuckles at this remembered line.*) Even for Shakespeare, the alternatives seem to be sovereign reason or madness. That's what I will do. I will put in the line from "Hamlet" and say, "Surely not. Surely those are not our alternatives. Surely many voices can and must be heard, voices which are neither mad nor sovereign." Isn't that what criticism is about, and dialogue, and civil society, both foreign and domestic? Enough.

Epilogue

James N. Rosenau

SAR, obviously in distress, moves furtively around his office. He pauses in front of his computer screen, moves to the window, then crosses over to a file and pulls out a folder, only to slam it on his desk and resume pacing. He seems to be in a continuous, anguished dialogue with himself, as if he is struggling with important decisions that he knows are bound to offend one or another of his colleagues. It would seem that his inclination to write an Epilogue highlighting the coherence underlying the several dialogues is in direct conflict with his analytic self, which tells him the dialogues do not readily lend themselves to the imposition of an overall structure. Furthermore, his phone is constantly ringing; his colleagues, aware that the time has come for him to complete the Epilogue, are asking tough questions about the future. He appreciates that the questions must be addressed, but at the same time he feels a strong obligation to probe what the convening of global voices has accomplished. Before he can start the probing, however, the phone begins to ring, bringing him back to his desk, where he irritably swings his chair to its usual position in front of the window, picks up the receiver, and gazes out across the campus. This view has always been calming for him, enabling him to be more responsive on the telephone, as if the movement of students between classes and the clusters that gather in intense conversation were visual reminders that the interplay of global voices is sustained by serious purposes.

SAR (*trying to sound relaxed*): Hello. SAR speaking.

SUKA: Oh, I'm so glad I found you in, SAR. I've been trying for several days.

SAR: Yes, I've been in and out. But what's up? These transatlantic calls are costly.

SUKA: Well, I gather you're working on the Epilogue, and I wondered how you're handling it. So much more has happened in the world since we completed and revised our dialogues that I'm concerned they may be obsolete.

SAR: I'm more concerned about whether we've achieved a coherent volume.

SUKA: That will take care of itself. But take your dialogue. It becomes increasingly obsolete as the U.S. role as the world's leader becomes increasingly questionable. You've acknowledged the loss of superpower status, but are you ready to concede that recent events have reduced the U.S. role to that of an ordinary country? The trade talks are stalled; Saddam Hussein is still in power; the former Soviet Union is in severe trouble; Czechoslovakia has broken up; a full-scale war is racking the former Yugoslavia; Somalians are starving to death by the thousands; and your political system seems paralyzed, unable to generate either the resources or the will needed to address any of these problems. It's as if the riots in Los Angeles were a portent of things to come.

SAR: It sounds like you're wondering whether the U.S. can become a superpower again, a kind of world policeman capable of imposing or sustaining a new world order.

SUKA: I guess I am. Your country seems so out of touch with its historic mission that I don't see how it can ever become a global policeman.

SAR: You know, JUSOFS would agree with you. He thinks the U.S. is in a long downhill slide. He argues that it has become more a multicultural regime than a melting pot, that it's a clumsy and erratic system that lacks shared values and thus can no longer move decisively or effectively on the world stage.

SUKA: I feel the same way about my own country. We English came to terms with our decline as a world power long ago, but we have yet to develop a consensus as to the new roles we should be playing in international affairs. Some of us are drawn toward Europe, and others are fearful of losing our identity in an integrated EC. So our political system is also paralyzed.

SAR: According to JUSOFS, the same is true of the French and the Italians. He insists that the Germans are also losing their way, that political paralysis prevails everywhere in the world. It's as if the new world order were largely a disorder.

SUKA: Why do you keep citing JUSOFS? It sounds like you're hiding behind him, SAR. What are your views on the decline of the U.S.? Are you as pessimistic as JUSOFS?

SAR: I ... (*He pauses, unsure of how to respond.*) I ... uh, well, I guess there's much to be said for his argument. On the other hand, even if the U.S. is in decline, its capabilities still exceed those of any other country. We can slide a long way down before it matters very much.

SUKA: You worry me, SAR. You seem so ambivalent. What has happened to your luxurious sense of being a superpower scholar?

SAR: Things have changed, SUKA, and I guess I have, too.

(*He lapses into silence.*)

SUKA: Well, good-bye, SAR. I hope you can work these things out. I'll be looking forward to seeing your Epilogue.

SAR (*mumbling, distracted*): How can we possibly achieve a coherent volume? An Epilogue is impossible!

(*He puts the telephone down, but it rings again immediately.*)

WESTFEM-TSITSI: Oh, SAR, I finally reached you. You're hard to find these days.

SAR: I know. But I've been working on the Epilogue for our volume. Somehow it really concerns me.

WESTFEM-TSITSI: I'm concerned about the impact of the end of the Cold War on the third world and how we can alert our readers to the dire circumstances that lie ahead.

SAR: What circumstances do you have in mind?

WESTFEM-TSITSI: I fear people aren't going to appreciate the extent to which suffering lies ahead in the absence of superpower competition in the third world. Neither publics nor governments in the industrial world care any more about poverty and famine in the Southern Hemisphere. They're so preoccupied with their own problems that they're ready to let history end in the third world. I mean literally end. The Somalian situation is a tragedy beyond description. There's no governance. And the situations in the Sudan and Afghanistan are about to descend to the same level of chaos. There's more. These are only the most obvious cases of what international neglect can lead to.

SAR: Have you any thoughts as to what can be done about the problem?

WESTFEM-TSITSI: We've got to keep the issues alive as best we can. The deterioration of economics and politics in the third world is so extensive, so utterly horrendous for people's daily lives, that it ought to be possible to reach and stir the consciences of students in the west.

SAR: That seems contradictory. First you say people don't care, and now you say they can be moved to action.

WESTFEM-TSITSI: It's not really a contradiction. People in the west are uncaring about the third world, but that doesn't mean their sensitivities can't be heightened and their energies mobilized. Look how far we've come in getting the world's women on the global agenda. There are still enormous obstacles to improving their circumstances, but the feminist movement has succeeded in transforming women's problems from nonissues into matters of real concern for both publics and governments.

SAR: Okay, let's say our students do become more sensitive to the horrors unfolding in the third world. What can they do then? Their stirred consciences are bound to be thwarted and lead to frustration and alienation, hardly a condition conducive to constructive action.

WESTFEM-TSITSI: No, SAR, you miss the point. Whenever publics

have been aroused in recent years, there have been consequences. Publics brought down the Wall in Berlin, forced
change in South Africa, and tumbled repressive governments
in all parts of the world. You know, SAR, you've been so detached as a superpower scholar that you've become oblivious
to the sources of change that are independent of U.S. foreign
policy.

SAR: You mean American scholars are part of the problem?

WESTFEM-TSITSI: I didn't say that, but I'm glad you did. You may be
changing, SAR.

SAR: Perhaps I am, along with everyone and everything else. (*He
subsides into mumbling again.*) This volume will never cohere.

(*WESTFEM-TSITSI, satisfied that SAR is willing to acknowledge
vulnerability, wishes him well and hangs up. It isn't long, however,
before SAR's musings are interrupted again by the ringing of the
telephone.*)

FATHER (AND SONS): Hey, SAR, how are you doing?

SAR: What's got into you? Joyfulness is not exactly your strong suit!

FATHER (AND SONS): We've been pondering whether the collapse
of the communist world has so discredited Marxism as to leave
the way clear for postmodernism to replace it as the dominant
radical critique, and we're persuaded that the likelihood of this
happening is very high.

SAR: You surprise me! I thought postmodernists were free of inclinations to prevail. And since when have you estimated likelihoods? A probability statement is a construction, but you guys
claim you only deal in deconstructions.

FATHER (AND SONS): A diversionary tactic, to say the least. Stick to
the question. Wouldn't you agree that the virtues of postmodern approaches have been brilliantly revealed by the quick demise of communist premises and thought?

SAR: Well, surely, something important has been revealed. For me
the demise of communism is more indicative of how tenuous
systems of thought really are than an argument for postmod-

ernism. Systems of thought may last seventy years, but they're nonetheless always on the edge of collapse. Once their foundations are shown to be faulty—once people break from their conceptual jails and see alternative ways of thinking and acting—the whole edifice can swiftly collapse.

FATHER (AND SONS): You are hopelessly empiricist!

SAR: No, the notion of system collapse is essentially a theoretical premise. It presumes that human systems are not immutable, that institutions are social constructions fashioned by people and repeated across time in response to historical experiences and immediate needs, and that consequently, such systems can undergo transformation when those who construct them see them for what they are.

FATHER (AND SONS): Okay, then you are hopelessly a theorist (even if in this instance there is some merit in your premise)!

SAR: Your agreement makes me nervous. It would be easier if we just said I am hopeless so that I can get back to pondering how to achieve a coherent volume out of our dialogues.

FATHER (AND SONS): What do you mean, "a coherent volume"?

SAR: One that makes the several dialogues appear part of the same enterprise. That's not easy, since our voices are so different.

(*MOTHER COURAGE enters.*)

MOTHER COURAGE: Rest easy, SAR. Coherence is an illusion. It runs against the order of things. Every voice has its own logic, its own story, and there is no reason why they need to be seen as related. You can't win; you'd be better off giving up on this "coherence" idea.

SAR: Did you say that coherence is against "the order of things"?

MOTHER COURAGE: Yes, it runs counter to the nature of people.

SAR: Isn't the nature of people a form of order?

MOTHER COURAGE: No, people are disorderly. There is no order!

SAR: Is not the absence of an order a form of order? If the post–Cold War world is chaotic, isn't that its order?

(*SAR chuckles to himself. Then, unimpressed with MOTHER COURAGE's reasoning, he tunes her out and quickly returns to pondering the problem of achieving a coherent volume. He half expects the phone to ring again precisely at the moment that it does. He even anticipates who is calling.*)

SAFS: Wow, has your line been busy. I was about to quit trying to reach you.

SAR: I know. All our colleagues have been calling. They want to talk about the chaotic state of world affairs and I …

SAFS: That's why I'm calling. I heard you were working on the Epilogue, and I want to urge you to follow Havel's lead and focus on the concept of "home."

SAR: My main concern is whether …

SAFS (*interrupting*): Even GORP was impressed with Havel's formulation. So it could be a unifying theme appropriate to the Epilogue.

SAR: Well, that's what I'm looking for. But only you and GORP pick up on it. The others move in very different directions, none of them overlapping. I fear a coherent volume may be beyond our grasp. "Home" can have so many diverse meanings.

SAFS: Look, all of us recognize that the old paradigms for comprehending international politics no longer work, that the world has been turned upside down by events that are not easily interpreted on the basis of conventional perspectives. But the concept of home, as Havel so succinctly elaborates it, can be at the core of any paradigm. You superpower scholars can use it to explain your shrinking power base, just as our English colleagues can think of their European orientations as an expansion of their home. And, of course, WESTFEM-TSITSI and I, much as our feminisms may be marked by different emphases, find common cause in the concept.

SAR: But go back and look at Havel's statement. He stressed that his Czechoslovakness was one of his homes. But Czechoslovakia has broken up. As of January 1993, it was no longer a home for anyone. The Czechs have their home and the Slovaks have theirs, but they do not have a common home.

SAFS: You miss the point, SAR. The beauty of Havel's thesis is that home is where you believe it to be. If the Slovaks no longer regard Czechoslovakia as home, then that is their reality. And when you consider the huge movements of people around the world, the mass emigrations, you realize that the meaning and location of home is a prime preoccupation of vast numbers of people. Today, it would seem, home is on wheels, in trucks, on carts, even a donkey's back.

SAR: I have the impression that Havel was trying to get at the stable sources of life in today's troubled world. For him, home involves the enduring commitments, the fixed locales, the permanent arrangements that are left behind when one moves across emotional and geographic borders.

SAFS: No, what counts are present commitments and arrangements, whatever the borders within which they may be located. They express the paradigm shifts that are so profoundly altering the conduct of world affairs. It was not until we allowed for parametric transformations, for the attenuation of enduring patterns and the evolution of new ones, that we could anticipate the authority crises that have weakened states, fostered the readiness of citizens to engage in collective action, and given new credence to the significance of the various "homes" to which Havel refers.

SAR: You'll get no argument from me on that. The more innovative conceptual equipment we can evolve, the better we'll be able to account for the vast changes that mark our time. There's a lot that calls for explanation, and I worry we'll rely too heavily on outworn modes of analysis.

SAFS: You seem to be a bundle of worries, SAR. All the changes seem to be eroding your confidence as a superpower scholar. It's as if you've collapsed into a brooding mood.

GORP (*briefly manifest*): It reminds me a lot of Havel. He's a brooder too.

SAR: No, Havel's broodings are about the human condition. My preoccupations are trivial by comparison.

SAFS: I'm concerned about you, SAR. There's no reason to be preoccupied with the coherence of our volume.

SAR: I know, but it's a matter of craft, of doing things right, and so I've been caught up in a dialogue with myself. I can't help it.

SAFS: Well, please know you have my support.

(*She waves him a warm good-bye. SAR's inner dialogue immediately takes over as he watches a cluster of students in the courtyard below gesturing heatedly at each other, obviously intensely involved in their own dialogue.*)

SAR'S EDITORIAL CONSCIENCE: Look, yield to your long-standing commitment to teasing out patterns and to the proposition that airing different voices will bring about convergence. Sure, there are some differences among the participants, but you're good at downplaying discordance. So just focus on the shared interest in entering a dialogue. Stress how seeing different perspectives is bound to lead to clarity.

SAR'S ANALYTIC CONSCIENCE: But I'm not so sure. Some of them go beyond difference. Some are saying we haven't achieved either convergence or clarity. TSITSI says my initial dialogue with JUSOFS amounted to "a dialogue of the deaf."

SAR'S EDITORIAL CONSCIENCE: That's absurd, and you know it! WESTFEM and TSITSI—and FATHER (AND SONS) too—clearly got sufficiently engaged by your superpower assertions to answer back. Deaf people don't hear and can't answer back. But your contributors did answer back.

SAR'S ANALYTIC CONSCIENCE: They sure did! But their answers amount to a rejection of the exercise. WESTFEM argues that our initial dialogue failed to involve "everyone listening and being partly transformed by the conversation," that it involved nothing more than "separate individuals with separate points of view trying to win by convincing others to change loyalties and identities."

SAR'S EDITORIAL CONSCIENCE: That's obviously false. Look at you.

The dialogue may not have transformed you, but it does seem to have given you pause in a number of ways.

SAR'S ANALYTIC CONSCIENCE: For instance?

SAR'S EDITORIAL CONSCIENCE: I sense you're not prepared to dismiss Der Derian's case for IR analysts living with heterogeneity rather than striving for elegant theory.

SAR'S ANALYTIC CONSCIENCE: Yes, but ...

SAR'S EDITORIAL CONSCIENCE: But what?

SAR'S ANALYTIC CONSCIENCE: But he also describes our dialogue as "ersatz," and he claims that my exchanges with JUSOFS are "a dialogue in only a formal sense, containing all kinds of double-talk and monological reasoning."

SAR'S EDITORIAL CONSCIENCE: That's just exaggeration. Allow him some poetic license. You know that you and JUSOFS did in fact join some important issues.

SAR'S ANALYTIC CONSCIENCE: There's another problem. How can I emphasize the coherence of the essays when only IRTS and SUKA went along with the original idea of starting immediately with a dialogue and then adding a second scene precipitated by questioning whether the end of the Cold War negates the original dialogue. Sylvester begins with a correspondence that seemingly involves two feminists, one a Western scholar and the other a Zimbabwean, but it turns out they are the same person and that each represents a part of Sylvester's own experience. This does not become evident until the second scene when they are in the same mental space on a flight to Harare and merge together in a single multifaceted identity. I can understand the significance of her being a "third-world-woman-first-world-feminist," but it may be perplexing for some readers who have never entertained the idea that scholars can have several identities as a consequence of engaging in scholarly pursuits that embed them in different cultures. Der Derian starts with an essay and then breaks his exchanges (note I didn't say his "dialogue") into three scenes with an epilogue essay of his own. And Elshtain ends with the reflections of an apparition. There's just no uniformity here!

SAR'S EDITORIAL CONSCIENCE: Relax. There's a lot to be said for this diversity. It occurs in a larger context that highlights, even brilliantly reveals, the very different ways IR scholars approach the subject. You should be pleased that they didn't adhere to your efforts to achieve uniformity. It would have been deadly dull!

SAR'S ANALYTIC CONSCIENCE: But readers want to have a sense that it all adds up. Many even want a conclusion that ends on an upbeat note, that celebrates the realization of common themes! That's why so many reviews of edited books rue the absence of a concluding chapter that ties all the contributions into a coherent whole and that thus demonstrates the wisdom of collecting the essays between the same covers.

SAR'S EDITORIAL CONSCIENCE: Well, make a virtue of the differences. Write an Epilogue that champions the success of your dialogues by championing their diversity.

SAR'S NORMATIVE CONSCIENCE: Let me get into this. You can make a case analytically for trumpeting diversity, but doing so would be to impose your own perspective in the guise of editorial prerogatives.

SAR'S EDITORIAL CONSCIENCE: What does that mean? Editors are supposed to tie things up in a conclusion that gives readers a sense of closure. Those are the rules of the game.

SAR'S NORMATIVE CONSCIENCE: No. To write an Epilogue is to strain for what may be a misleading sense of closure. It amounts to having the last word, just like superpowers do. They use all kinds of guises to impose their outlooks in such a way that they seem to be merely playing by the rules.

SAR'S EDITORIAL CONSCIENCE: Not at all. If you call attention to the diversity of the essays, you can hardly be accused of imposing a perspective. I'm afraid your lean-over-backward-to-be-fair syndrome—your impulse to deny, in effect, that you enjoy the luxuries of a superpower orientation—is blinding you to the basic requirements of an edited volume.

SAR'S NORMATIVE CONSCIENCE: But what about Der Derian's observation that the chance of these dialogues contributing to new thinking about IR "probably depends most on just how jealous each is of the right to the last word"? He may be right, you know.

SAR'S EDITORIAL CONSCIENCE: You're impossible! So wishy-washy, so ready to avoid your superpower obligations!

SAR'S ANALYTIC CONSCIENCE: No. Here my normative and analytic impulses converge. Normatively, an epilogue is the last word and, as such, it does impose. And analytically, I'm not so sure that I can highlight the diversity without implying an underlying coherence that readers may mistake for conclusions shared by all the contributors and their characters. I just can't fake it!

SAR'S EDITORIAL CONSCIENCE: Okay, then why don't you bring their characters into the dialogue?!

SAR'S NORMATIVE CONSCIENCE: You mean put words in their mouths?

SAR'S EDITORIAL CONSCIENCE: WESTFEM and IRTS brought you into their dialogues. Why not give voice to them here?

SAR'S NORMATIVE CONSCIENCE: Because they'll see it as a power play, just another case of an American using his strategic advantage as editor to make sure the materials are consistent with his interpretation.

SAR'S EDITORIAL CONSCIENCE: But you do have some interpretations, don't you? After all, several of the dialogues make SAR seem pretty foolish. You're entitled to argue back, you know.

SAR'S ANALYTIC CONSCIENCE: But these are my friends. I like IRTS, and I can even put up with SUKA. And WESTFEM and TSITSI are really good people, even if their feminist-colored glasses skew their views of people like me. I'm not sure I grasp all the postmodern characters, but they do make a number of valuable observations from which I can't really dissent.

SAR'S EDITORIAL CONSCIENCE: Some analyst you are. Just because they're your friends doesn't mean you can't differ with them! And your norms are way off, too. In effect, you're saying that because you like them—because you want to retain your friendship with them—you're disinclined to assert your own point of view or use your position as editor of the volume to give some direction to it.

SAR'S NORMATIVE CONSCIENCE: Is that what I'm saying?

SAR'S EDITORIAL CONSCIENCE: I think so. Is that how you actually feel about it?

SAR'S NORMATIVE CONSCIENCE: Sort of. I also feel that we who are superpower scholars need to demonstrate some open-mindedness and recognize that subsequent generations may have worthy viewpoints.

SAR'S EDITORIAL CONSCIENCE: Are you willing to give up your own analytic judgments just to maintain a balanced dialogue and to avoid putting people down with your own firm conclusions?

SAR'S NORMATIVE CONSCIENCE: But they won't be able to answer back. It seems unfair.

SAR'S EDITORIAL CONSCIENCE: Do you think if they were doing the editing, they'd shy away from conclusions because that would be unfair?

SAR'S NORMATIVE CONSCIENCE: Of course they would.

SAR'S EDITORIAL CONSCIENCE: I don't know, SAR. How'd you ever get this far being so unwilling to step on a few toes?

SAR'S NORMATIVE CONSCIENCE: You don't understand.

SAR'S EDITORIAL CONSCIENCE: I think I do! Why don't you compromise by giving voice to their characters and then answering back in your voice?

SAR'S NORMATIVE CONSCIENCE: That could be unfair too. I could easily load the interchange in my favor.

SAR'S EDITORIAL CONSCIENCE: You really are impossible! Look, books have to end. There just have to be a few last pages. Let them be yours. Bring this dialogue to a meaningful close.

SAR'S ANALYTIC CONSCIENCE: You're right! We can't go on like this.

SAR'S EDITORIAL CONSCIENCE: Now, that's better. Let me get you started. What do you think WESTFEM-TSITSI are trying to say, and do you agree with them?

JUSOFS (*entering*): Wait, let me start. SAR can't be afraid of putting words into *my* mouth. After all, I'm SAR's creation in the first place.

SAR'S NORMATIVE CONSCIENCE: You're right. There's no discomfort in ascribing views to you. Go ahead, JUSOFS, I'm ready to hear (and write) you.

JUSOFS: I just wanted to go back to the question of your power as a superpower scholar. In our original dialogue, I contested your denial that you were endowed with any special powers, and all the others seem to agree with me that high-status American academics use their clout to dominate the field, decide what concepts are acceptable, prevent the acquisition of legitimacy by alternative formulations, accord salience to particular studies, highlight the worth of particular journals, and so on. IRTS goes on at length about how "serious U.K. academics have little choice but to follow the lead" of their American IR counterparts and how the latter pay little attention to research being conducted elsewhere in the world. Likewise, WESTFEM and TSITSI expound on how the "chorus of masculine voices"—what they also call "the mainstream of IR"—in the U.S. is inhibiting, if not preventing, the inroads of feminist perspectives. And Der Derian's "hybrid dialogue" is pervaded with implications that your "*ersatz* dialogue" is designed "to preempt criticisms" and is thus "yet another arbitrary delimitation of intellectual options," which, nonetheless, has "injunctive power" and perpetuates "the enclosure acts of ... dialogues in IR." SAFS, too, talks critically of closure, particularly what she calls "grand narratives of closure."

SAR'S ANALYTIC CONSCIENCE: Ah, but SAFS rues any such narratives, "whether feminist, nonfeminist, antifeminist, political economy, rational choice, realist, neorealist."

JUSOFS: But she also cites with approval what I said in our first dialogue about you and your peers—what she calls "the academic arm of the powers-that-be"—saying that it is inextricably "hooked into the interstate system."

SAR'S ANALYTIC CONSCIENCE: Well, let me say …

JUSOFS (*interrupting*): So there you have it, SAR, all of us view the research of senior superpower scholars as the exercise of power. What do you say to that?

SAR'S ANALYTIC CONSCIENCE: I don't attach any importance to it. If I thought leaders in the public arena took us seriously, pondered our findings, wrestled with our axioms, considered our analyses, then maybe I'd agree that, unbeknownst to ourselves, we are exercising power. But I've long had the impression that no one in the policy community reads or listens. Our voices peter out once they leave the ivory tower.

JUSOFS: But within the ivory tower, your generation has no hesitation about flexing its muscles. You've even done it here.

SAR'S ANALYTIC CONSCIENCE: That's absurd. Give me one example.

JUSOFS: You're having the last word in writing this Epilogue. There's a lot of power lodged in doing so.

SAR'S EDITORIAL CONSCIENCE: But all collections of essays need a concluding chapter. I prevailed over my analytic conscience to do this Epilogue. No one can really complain, moreover, because the Epilogue alerts readers to the dangers of being skewed by those who have the last word. So that's a weak example, JUSOFS. You must have a better one.

JUSOFS: As a matter of fact, I do. You exercised your editorial prerogatives and altered the format WESTFEM-TSITSI used to label themselves in their dialogue. In their original ISA paper, they used lowercase for themselves. You capitalized them. That's an arbitrary exercise of power!

SAR'S EDITORIAL CONSCIENCE: That was done to achieve a measure of uniformity across the dialogues.

JUSOFS: Don't kid yourself. It's still an arbitrary exercise of power!

SAR'S ANALYTIC CONSCIENCE: No, my editorial conscience is wrong. I capitalized their names for a different reason. As I understand it, they used lowercase for themselves and uppercase for JUSOFS and myself as a way of highlighting the subordinate position of feminist scholars, whereas I wanted to stress that this is erroneous, that they are the equal of (and, in some instances, even superior to) their male colleagues.

JUSOFS: It's still an arbitrary act of power. You didn't consult them about it, did you?

SAR'S EDITORIAL CONSCIENCE: No.

JUSOFS: There you are. Your last word really does prevail.

SAR'S EDITORIAL CONSCIENCE: Wait, let WESTFEM and TSITSI issue their own challenges.

SAR'S ANALYTIC CONSCIENCE: Can't we just stop here? I've already put my friendships at risk.

SAR'S EDITORIAL CONSCIENCE: No, you owe them a hearing. So go ahead, WESTFEM-TSITSI. The ball is in your court.[1]

(*WESTFEM enters.*)

WESTFEM: We need to straighten out this uppercase-lowercase business. The reason for the lowercase in our discussion was to highlight an important substantive point, namely, that IR doesn't need another heroic uppercase discourse, dialogue, or set of theories. We don't need to give any particular speaker so much credit for being "the" spokesperson for "the" position, "the" expert, "the big shot." That you interpret the lowercase usage as a sign that we want to highlight dominance and subordination is an interesting mirror of your own understanding of the issue.

SAR'S ANALYTIC CONSCIENCE: I don't know about that. But if the lowercase is an important symbol to you, then I want to honor it. Go ahead, give voice to the conclusions you'd like to leave with the readers.

westfem: I've been trying to stress, demonstrate, reveal, or otherwise clarify how you and other senior IR scholars in the mainstream of the field subsume women and our characteristic assignments into a false humanism of elite men or of ordinary masculinism.

SAR'S ANALYTIC CONSCIENCE: It's true that my understanding of politics at all levels has never allowed for the possibility that gender differences matter. I see people as seeking dignity, vindication, power, prestige, and a host of other goals, but I haven't presumed that differences between men and women account for significant amounts of the variance in how such goals are sought or how the issues are framed. Maybe there are differences, but like health and vocational factors, they don't strike me as accounting for enough of the variabilities in politics to warrant systematic attention.

westfem: You continue to make my point better than I ever could.

tsitsi: I would add that when the activities of ordinary people are mentioned in mainstream writings, they're rarely discussed as crosscut by race and gender. When I say "ordinary people," I mean people like me in Zimbabwe.

SAR'S ANALYTIC CONSCIENCE: Let me put it differently. Even if gender orientations differ and lead to different forms of political behavior, some men have female orientations and some women have male orientations, which thus again blurs any variabilities that might be attributed to gender distinctions.

westfem: Come on, my friend, you're missing the point again. You suggest that some men can have the biological orientations of females and some women can have male biological orientations. Fine. But exactly what do you mean by this?

SAR'S ANALYTIC CONSCIENCE: Well, you're the one who referred to a "male-bodied person" as if that were a significant category of being.

westfem: Ah, but the context for that comment was the empirical fact that mostly male bodies are circulating through the positions of state leadership in the "new" countries of the world. Can you justify that fact simply by arguing that some male bodies can be like "women," so we don't ever need to have female bodies in positions of power? Is this not an excuse for keeping things as they are under the guise of relieving all of "us" of the burden of gender?

SAR'S ANALYTIC CONSCIENCE: But I don't call myself SAMS (Senior

American Masculine Scholar). Perhaps I didn't want to confuse things by calling myself SAFS. One gendered senior scholar is enough, and even SAFS expresses gratitude to SICC "for relieving [her] of the burden of gender!"

(*SAFS enters.*)

SAFS: No wait, I only want to …

SAR'S ANALYTIC CONSCIENCE: Don't back away, SAFS, you did say that.

SAFS (*speechless*): Uh …

westfem: You can hide behind your senior colleague, SAR, but I won't let you off so easy. You haven't called yourself SAMS because you take gender for granted. Again, that makes my point: It's an omission that expresses a sense of superiority, a power trip that treats people as irrelevant.

SAR'S ANALYTIC CONSCIENCE: Look, my research into gender differences based on solid empirical data has yielded a null finding,[2] and my theoretical formulations yielded a whole book that stresses the importance of microphenomena—that is, the activities of ordinary people.[3]

tsitsi: You're playing with words! It feels like you're attacking us.

SAR'S NORMATIVE CONSCIENCE: She's right! You're purposely misconstruing their central idea.

SAR'S ANALYTIC CONSCIENCE: No, I only want to point out that human affairs, and world politics in particular, are too complex, too much the product of a multiplicity of sources, to justify a paradigm founded on what is essentially a single explanatory variable.

SAR'S EDITORIAL CONSCIENCE (*a bit uncomfortable at having pressed SAR'S ANALYTIC CONSCIENCE to speak out*): Um, maybe we should shift …

westfem-tsitsi: Wait, we'd like the last word on this. You're hiding behind complexity, SAR. Sure the world is extraordinarily complicated, pervaded with causal webs, racked by diversity; but that does not negate the perspective we're advancing. We're not saying a feminist IR would uncover simplicities. We're only arguing that alternative perspectives and paradigms are possible and that this "space for maneuver" can usefully be explored to the benefit of all.

SAR'S ANALYTIC CONSCIENCE: That's what I'm arguing too. But you can't hear me. Whatever position I take, you interpret it as gender dominated.

westfem-tsitsi: There you go again. You just can't let us have the last word, can you?

SAR'S ANALYTIC CONSCIENCE: But it's true. You suggest that any new theory I might eke out to explain the complexity may be only "a novel form of masculine voice." It feels like a no-win situation. Like the tango, it takes two to have a dialogue of the deaf.

westfem-tsitsi: Okay, my friend, we'll get a hearing aid. Will you?

SAR'S ANALYTIC CONSCIENCE: Sure, I …

SAR'S EDITORIAL CONSCIENCE: Good, let's leave it there! (*pause*) Let's shift the focus. What about IRTS and SUKA? Do you have any major quarrel with their argument?

SAR'S ANALYTIC CONSCIENCE: You've goaded me enough. I want to stop here. These are my friends, remember. We're all hearing-aided, human-bodied people.

(*IRTS enters.*)

IRTS: Hold on, SAR, you're not getting off that easy. I'll grant that you're open to new theorizing, but you're still a positivist, still hoping to uncover a single reality, even if you do so with a new paradigm.

SAR'S ANALYTIC CONSCIENCE: What's wrong with that?

IRTS: I told you. You talk "as if knowledge is some kind of representation of reality, whereas it's really an interpretation of it, and never complete at that."

SAR'S ANALYTIC CONSCIENCE: Of course, any representation is nothing other than an interpretation. I don't differ with that at all. Indeed, that's all science is. It consists of ever-changing consensuses (or, sometimes, dissensuses) among observers as to how one or another aspect of world politics has functioned, does function, or will function. Scientific theories and findings can never be more than integrated probability statements, and the goal is to improve on the probabilities, not to demonstrate a final, absolute, and immutable representation of reality.

IRTS: No, you misunderstand the point. The point is that ... there are *always* [at least] two distinct stories to tell.

SAR'S ANALYTIC CONSCIENCE: I'd rephrase that: There are always at least two sets of competing probability statements, since we can never aspire to explaining or understanding 100 percent of the variance.

IRTS: There you go again. Now you're playing with my words. There's an absolute difference here!

SAR'S ANALYTIC CONSCIENCE: I can't respond to that. If you're going to pose absolutes, then we really are on different wavelengths.

IRTS: It's just a figure of speech.

SAR'S ANALYTIC CONSCIENCE: I wonder. Without even making a systematic search, I identified five times in your dialogue when you used the word "totally" and another four times when you used "absolutely." At one point you even asserted that you "totally believe" that American IR scholars are led by the U.S. policy agenda.

IRTS: Well, you are!

SAR'S ANALYTIC CONSCIENCE: Be that as it may—and I think you exaggerate, as I tried to tell JUSOFS in our original go-around—it's nonetheless worrying that your perspective is cast in terms of "totallies," "completelies," and "absolutelies." It sounds like you're not sure of your own observations and convictions, else why do you need to bulwark them with such adjectival prefaces?

IRTS: As I say, these are just figures of speech.

SAR'S ANALYTIC CONSCIENCE: But don't they prevent you from discerning, much less relating, the two or more stories you say are always at work?

SUKA: That's exactly right!

(*SUKA enters.*)

IRTS: Keep quiet, you fool. There are no "exactlies" either!

SAR'S ANALYTIC CONSCIENCE: Ah, now we're back on the same wavelength.

SAR'S EDITORIAL CONSCIENCE: Good, let's leave it there and move on to ...

IRTS: Wait, he (or are you a she?) hasn't responded to the point about IR scholars in the U.S. being prey to, even victims of, their country's policy agenda.

SAR'S ANALYTIC CONSCIENCE: I addressed that with JUSOFS. So I'll just repeat that you've overstated the point. Sure, some of my colleagues have been funded by my government, and sure, some may subconsciously allow our mass media to frame the issues for them, but there are also many who pride themselves on their readiness to contest what they perceive as the received wisdom. Remember, there are always at least two stories.

IRTS: You got me there. But come on, SAR, are you saying that many of you Americans are free of nationalist orientations, that you're truly detached observers, that a global social science is possible?

SAR'S ANALYTIC CONSCIENCE: I wish!

SAR'S NORMATIVE CONSCIENCE: I wish for that, too!

SAR'S EDITORIAL CONSCIENCE: And so do I!

IRTS: Well, now there's some agreement. But, aside from your wishes, how would you characterize the impact of national factors on your colleagues today?

SAR'S ANALYTIC CONSCIENCE: I'd say that we're a bit at loose ends. We know our status as superpower scholars has come to an end, but we don't quite know how to proceed from here.

IRTS: Would you like a suggestion?

SAR'S ANALYTIC CONSCIENCE: Sure.

IRTS: Turn more of your attention to scholarship being undertaken elsewhere in the world.

SAR'S ANALYTIC CONSCIENCE: I accept that.

SAR'S EDITORIAL CONSCIENCE: Good, now we can move on to your responses to all those parents (and their children) and pets (and their meals).

SAR'S ANALYTIC CONSCIENCE: I'd only say that, if any theory, even those expressing "righteous anger," is as good (or as bad) as any other theory, as those characters propose, then any theories that I or my peers may advance are equally interesting. If there's no meaning other than what language can fashion, then our theories are as meaningless as anyone else's.

(*FATHER AND [SONS] enter.*)

FATHER: But you've already said you're impressed by the "*necessity* of heterogeneity for understanding ourselves and others."

SAR'S ANALYTIC CONSCIENCE: Yes, but that doesn't require me to treat all the competing theories as equal and avoid prioritizing them.

(*MOTHER COURAGE enters.*)

MOTHER COURAGE: Ugh, do you have to use such words?

SAR'S ANALYTIC CONSCIENCE: No, but I have to have some way of differentiating among the various paradigms.

FATHER (AND SONS): Don't try. I assure you, your "disciplinary conformity" will get you through.

SAR'S NORMATIVE CONSCIENCE: No, I see myself as a nonconformist!

SAR'S ANALYTIC CONSCIENCE: Me too!

SAR'S EDITORIAL CONSCIENCE: And so do I!

(*DOG enters.*)

DOG: Now that's the beef!

sar's editorial conscience: Hooray! More agreement. That leaves SAFS and SICC: Have you a reaction to them?

sar's analytic conscience: You know, I really don't—just positive feelings that both of them have deep insights and compelling perspectives. I like that SICC relieves SAFS of "the burden of gender," that SAFS resists "a collapse into empathy," that she seeks to account "for difference and variation—not simply remark on it or 'leave space' for it." Wow, all that makes a lot of sense to me.

sar's editorial conscience: Good. Let's end it there.

westfem-tsitsi: Yes, let's.

irts: I'm willing.

jusofs: So am I.

suka: But chaps ... (*He notes everyone staring at him.*) ... Well, okay ...

parents (and children): No argument here.

dog: Woof!

sar's normative conscience: We've done it! We've achieved a modicum of coherence!

sar's editorial conscience: Whew!

Notes

Prologue

1. E. H. Carr, *What Is History?* (Harmondsworth, England: Penguin Books, 1964), p. 42.

2. See, for example, the various essays in Robert O. Keohane, ed., *Neorealism and Its Critics* (New York: Columbia University Press, 1986), especially the chapters by Richard K. Ashley and Robert G. Gilpin.

Act I

1. Axel Dorscht, "What Realism Really Does: A Deconstruction of International Relations," a paper presented at the annual meeting of the American Political Science Association, Washington, D.C., September 1–4, 1988, p. 1.

2. Ibid., p. 4.

3. For some of the early findings generated by the CREON project, see Maurice A. East, Stephen A. Salmore, and Charles F. Hermann, eds., *Why Nations Act: Theoretical Perspectives for Comparative Foreign Policy Studies* (Beverly Hills: Sage Publications, 1978). Early results from the leadership surveys are available in Ole R. Holsti and James N. Rosenau, *American Leadership in World Affairs: The Breakdown of Consensus* (London and Winthrop, MA: George Allen & Unwin, 1984).

4. Ekkehart Krippendorf, "The Dominance of American Approaches in International Relations," *Millennium* 16 (Summer 1987): 212.

5. Ibid.

6. See, for example, Robert Axelrod, *The Evolution of Cooperation* (New York: Basic Books, 1984); David A. Baldwin, *Economic Statecraft* (Princeton: Princeton University Press, 1985); Robert O. Keohane, *After Hegemony: Cooperation and Discord in the World Political Economy* (Princeton: Princeton University Press, 1984); and Stephen D. Krasner, ed., *International Regimes* (Ithaca: Cornell University Press, 1983).

7. James N. Rosenau, *The Dramas of Politics: An Introduction to the Joys of Inquiry* (Boston: Little Brown, 1973), pp. 236–238.

8. Dorscht, "What Realism Really Does," p. 4.

9. Cf. Hans J. Morgenthau, *Politics Among Nations: The Struggle for Power and Peace,* 5th ed. (New York: Alfred A. Knopf, 1973); Arnold Wolfers, *Discord and Collaboration: Essays on International Politics* (Baltimore: Johns Hopkins University Press, 1962); and Kenneth N. Waltz, *Theory of International Politics* (Reading, MA: Addison-Wesley, 1979).

10. Morgenthau, *Politics Among Nations,* p. 5

11. Hedley Bull, "International Theory: The Case for a Classical Approach," *World Politics* 19 (April 1966): 361–377.

12. Dorscht, "What Realism Really Does," p. 5.

13. Ibid.

14. Robert C. North, "Research Pluralism and the International Elephant," in K. Knorr and J. N. Rosenau, eds., *Contending Approaches to International Politics* (Princeton: Princeton University Press, 1969), p. 218.

15. Krippendorf, "The Dominance of American Approaches," p. 213 (italics in original).

16. James N. Rosenau, "Pre-Theories and Theories of Foreign Policy," in R. B. Farrell, ed., *Approaches to Comparative and International Politics* (Evanston: Northwestern University Press, 1966), pp. 27–92.

17. Krippendorf, "The Dominance of American Approaches," p. 213.

18. Ibid., p. 214 (italics in original).

19. Ibid.

20. See, for example, James Der Derian and Michael J. Shapiro, eds., *International/Intertextual Relations: Postmodern Readings of World Politics* (Lexington, MA: Lexington Books, 1989); Symposium, "Philosophical Traditions in International Relations," *Millennium* 17 (Summer 1988): 189–348; and Pauline Rosenau, "Once Again into the Fray: International Relations Confronts the Humanities," *Millennium* 19 (March 1990): 83–110.

21. Illustrative in this regard is Paul Kennedy, *The Rise and Fall of Great Powers: Economic Change and Military Conflict from 1500 to 2000* (New York: Random House, 1987).

22. Bruce Russett, "The Mysterious Case of Vanishing Hegemony; or, Is Mark Twain Really Dead?" *International Organization* 39 (Spring 1985): 207–232; Samuel P. Huntington, "The U.S.—Decline or Renewal?" *Foreign Affairs* 67 (Winter 1988/1989): 76–96.

23. James N. Rosenau, "Before Cooperation: Hegemons, Regimes, and Habit-Driven Actors in World Politics," *International Organization* 40 (Autumn 1986): 884–885.

24. Ibid., pp. 885–886.

25. James N. Rosenau, *Turbulence in World Politics: A Theory of Change and Continuity* (Princeton: Princeton University Press, 1990), pp. 454–459.

Act II

I prepared the first draft of this chapter in 1990 while I was a senior associate member of St. Antony's College, University of Oxford. I revised it a year later at the University of Southern California, where I was a senior visiting scholar at the Center for International Studies. I thank both institutions for the time they provided me to think and to write. And I thank my Zimbabwean friends—for everything.

1. Jane Flax, "Postmodernism and Gender Relations in Feminist Theory," *Signs* 12, no. 4 (1987): 629.

2. Jean Elshtain, *Women and War* (Brighton: Wheatsheaf, 1987); Cynthia Enloe, *Bananas, Beaches and Bases: Making Feminist Sense of International Politics* (London: Pandora, 1989) and *Does Khaki Become You? The Militarisation of Women's Lives* (London: Pluto, 1983); Sara Ruddick, "Pacifying the Forces: Drafting Women in the Interests of Peace," *Signs* 8, no. 3 (1983): 471–489; Sharon MacDonald, P. Holdern, and S. Ardener, eds., *Images of Women in Peace and War: Cross-Cultural and Historical Perspectives* (Madison: University of Wisconsin Press, 1988); E. Croll, *Feminism and Socialism in China* (London: Routledge and Kegan Paul, 1978); J. Nash and H. Safa, eds., *Women and Change in Latin America* (South Hadley, MA: Bergin and Harvey, 1986); Jane Parpart and Kathleen Staudt, *Women and the State in Africa* (Boulder: Lynne Rienner, 1989); Maria Mies, *Patriarchy and Accumulation on a World Scale: Women in the International Division of Labor* (London: Zed, 1986). Also see *Millennium* 17, no. 3 (1988), a special issue on women in international relations.

3. Yosef Lapid, "The Third Debate: On the Prospects of International Theory in a Post-Positivist Era," *International Studies Quarterly* 33, no. 3 (1989): 235–254; Paul Viotti and Mark Kauppi, *International Relations Theory: Realism, Pluralism and Globalism* (London: Macmillan, 1987); K. Holsti, *The Dividing Discipline* (Winchester, MA: Allen and Unwin, 1985).

4. James N. Rosenau, "Superpower Scholars: Sensitive, Submissive, or Self-Deceptive?" a paper presented at the annual meeting of the International Studies Association, Washington, D.C., April 1980, p. 11.

5. *Sjamboks* are police sticks.

6. Joan Kelly, "Did Women Have A Renaissance?" in Catharine Stimpson, ed., *Women, History, and Theory: The Essays of Joan Kelly* (Chicago: University of Chicago Press, 1984), pp. 19–50.

7. Zimbabwe attained independence from Great Britain and from local Rhodesian settler rule in 1980 after nearly a decade of a multicentered armed struggle in which women figured prominently. For further discussion, see Christine Sylvester, "'Urban Women Cooperators,' 'Progress,'

and 'African Feminism in Zimbabwe,'" *Differences: A Journal of Feminist Cultural Studies* 3, no. 1 (1991): 39–62.

8. Thomas Schelling, *Arms and Influence* (New Haven: Yale University Press, 1966), p. 134.

9. Bruce Russett, "The Real Decline in Nuclear Hegemony," in Ernst-Otto Czempiel and James Rosenau, eds., *Global Changes and Theoretical Challenges: Approaches to World Politics in the 1990s* (Lexington, MA: Lexington Books, 1989), p. 185.

10. See, for instance, R.B.J. Walker, "Gender and Critique in the Theory of International Relations," and Jean Elshtain, "Sovereignty, Identity, Sacrifice," in V. Spike Peterson, ed., *Gendered States: Feminist (Re)Visions of International Relations Theory* (Boulder: Lynne Rienner, 1992). Also, Richard Ashley, "Living on Border Lines: Man, Poststructuralism, and War," in James Der Derian and Michael Shapiro, eds., *International/Intertextual Relations: Postmodern Readings of World Politics* (Lexington, MA: Lexington Books, 1989), pp. 259–321.

11. This is an equation Richard Ashley makes in "Living on Border Lines."

12. See the discussion of feminist standpoint theory in Nancy Hirschmann, "Freedom, Recognition, and Obligation: A Feminist Approach to Political Theory," *American Political Science Review* 83, no. 4 (1989): 1227–1244; Christine Sylvester, "The Emperors' Theories and Transformations: Looking at the Field Through Feminist Lenses," in Dennis Pirages and Christine Sylvester, eds., *Transformations in the Global Political Economy* (London: Macmillan Press, 1990), pp. 230–253; and Robert Keohane, "International Relations Theory: Contributions of a Feminist Standpoint," *Millennium* 18, no. 2 (1989): 245–253.

13. Carol Gilligan, *In A Different Voice: Psychological Theory and Women's Development* (Cambridge: Harvard University Press, 1982). See comments on the morality of care by Joan Tronto, "Beyond Gender Difference to a Theory of Care," *Signs* 12, no. 4 (1987): 644–663.

14. Enloe, *Bananas, Beaches and Bases*, p. 13.

15. See discussion of property rights in a community in John Ruggie, "International Structure and International Transformation: Space, Time, and Method," in Czempiel and Rosenau, eds., *Global Changes and Theoretical Challenges*, pp. 21–36.

16. For further discussion of patriarchal peace, see Christine Sylvester, "Patriarchy, Peace, and Women Warriors," in Linda Forcey, ed., *Peace: Meanings, Politics, Strategies* (New York: Praeger Press, 1989), pp. 97–112.

17. Enloe, *Bananas, Beaches and Bases*, p. 17.

18. Filomina Chioma Steady, "African Feminism: A Worldwide Perspective," in Roasalyn Terborg-Penn, S. Harley, and A. B. Rusing, eds.,

Women in Africa and the African Diaspora (Washington: Howard University Press, 1987), pp. 8, 20.

19. Sekai Nzenza, *Zimbabwean Woman: My Own Story* (London: Karia Press, 1988), p. 153.

20. Czempiel and Rosenau, eds., *Global Changes and Theoretical Challenges.*

21. Mies, *Patriarchy and Accumulation on a World Scale;* Enloe, *Bananas, Beaches and Bases.*

22. Ruggie, "Structure and Transformation," p. 32.

23. Elshtain, *Women and War,* p. 222.

24. James Rosenau, "Global Changes and Theoretical Challenges: Toward a Postinternational Politics for the 1990s," in Czempiel and Rosenau, eds., *Global Changes and Theoretical Challenges,* p. 10, commenting on the contribution by John Ruggie, "Structure and Transformation."

25. Salman Rushdie, "In Good Faith," *The Independent,* London, February 4, 1990, p. 18.

26. Thomas J. Biersteker, "Critical Reflections on Post-Positivism in International Relations," *International Studies Quarterly* 33, no. 3 (1989): 266.

27. Kathleen Jones, "The Trouble with Authority," *Differences: A Journal of Feminist Cultural Studies* 3, no. 1 (1991): 122.

28. Rosenau, "Global Changes and Theoretical Challenges," p. 3. Also, James N. Rosenau, *Turbulence in World Politics: A Theory of Continuity and Change* (Princeton: Princeton University Press, 1990).

29. See *International Studies Quarterly* 34, no. 3 (1990), a special issue on "Speaking the Language of Exile: Dissidence in International Studies."

30. Peter Katzenstein, "International Relations Theory and the Analysis of Change," in Czempiel and Rosenau, eds., *Global Changes and Theoretical Challenges,* p. 293.

31. See Bradley Klein, "After Strategy: The Search for a Post-Modern Politics of Peace," *Alternatives* 13, no. 3 (1988): 293–318.

32. See, for instance, Richard Falk, Samuel Kim, and Saul Mendlovitz, eds., *Towards a Just World Order* (Boulder: Westview Press, 1982).

33. E.g., Czempiel and Rosenau, eds., *Global Changes and Theoretical Challenges,* and Rosenau, *Turbulence in World Politics.* "Our" analyses merit one quick mention only in Yale H. Ferguson and Richard W. Mansbach, "Between Celebration and Despair: Constructive Suggestions for Future International Theory," *International Studies Quarterly* 35, no. 4 (1991): 364.

34. See related discussion in Christine Sylvester, "Simultaneous Revolutions: The Zimbabwean Case," *Journal of Southern African Studies* 6,

no. 3 (1990): 452–475; also, Christine Sylvester, "Continuity and Disconti-
nuity in Zimbabwe's Development History," *African Studies Review* 28,
no. 1 (1985): 19–44.

35. "Working Paper Defining Our Position: Women's Initiative: Lila Offensive," *Frauen in die Offensive* (Berlin: Dietz Verlag, 1990).

36. Jane Flax, *Thinking Fragments: Psychoanalysis, Feminism, and
Postmodernism in the Contemporary West* (Berkeley: University of California Press, 1989), pp. 225–226.

37. See discussion in Christine Sylvester, *Feminist Theory and International Relations in a Postmodern Era* (Cambridge: Cambridge University
Press, forthcoming 1994), Chapter 1.

38. Kathy Ferguson and Kirstie McClure, "Politics/Power/Culture:
Postmodernity and Feminist Political Theory," *Differences: A Journal of
Feminist Cultural Studies* 3, no. 1 (1991): iii.

39. See Christine Sylvester, "Some Dangers of Merging Feminist and
Peace Projects," *Alternatives* 8, no. 4 (1987): 493–510.

40. Linda Nicholson, ed., *Feminism/Postmodernism* (London:
Routledge: 1990), p. 3.

41. Gwyn Kirk, "Our Greenham Common: Feminism and Nonvio-
lence," in Adrienne Harris and Ynestra King, eds., *Rocking the Ship of
State: Toward a Feminist Peace Politics* (Boulder: Westview, 1989), p. 117.
Also see discussion in Christine Sylvester, "Feminists and Realists Look at
Autonomy and Obligation in International Relations," in Peterson, ed.,
Gendered States: Feminist (Re)Visions of International Relations Theory.

42. See discussion of liberal dialogues in Nancy Hirschmann, *Rethink-
ing Obligation: A Feminist Method for Political Theory* (Ithaca: Cornell
University Press, 1992).

43. Flax, *Thinking Fragments*, p. 233.

44. Ibid.

45. For a discussion of these forces, see Sylvester, "Unities and
Disunities in Zimbabwe's 1990 Election," *Journal of Modern African Studies* 28, no. 3(1990): 375–400. Also, Christine Sylvester, *Zimbabwe: The Political Economy of Contradictory Development* (Boulder: Westview Press,
1991).

46. By analogy with Gayatri Spivak's point in "Can the Subaltern
Speak?" in Cary Nelson and Lawrence Grossberg, eds., *Marxism and the
Interpretation of Culture* (Urbana, IL: University of Illinois Press, 1988),
pp. 271–313. Do people with powerful identities constantly speak only of
themselves when they think they are representing others with lesser
power? Do we faculty debaters reinforce subordination, and our own
agendas, when we speak of "graduate students"? Can "men" ever represent "women"? Can postmodernist "men" represent "feminists"? Or do

many of us have hyphenated selves-memories that enable subaltern identities to speak?

47. See Sylvester, "The Emperors' Theories and Transformations."

48. Ruddick, "Pacifying the Forces."

49. Maria Lugones, "Playfulness, 'World'-Travelling, and Loving Perception," in Gloria Anzaldua, ed., *Making Face, Making Soul—Haciendo Caras: Creative and Critical Perspectives by Women of Color* (San Francisco: Aunt Lute, 1990), p. 396.

Act III

1. Paul Kennedy, *The Rise and Fall of the Great Powers* (London: Unwin Hyman, 1988).

2. Francis Fukuyama, "The End of History?" *The National Interest,* no. 16 (Summer 1989): 3–18.

3. Michael Cox, "From Detente to the 'New Cold War': The Crisis of the Cold War System," *Millennium* 13, no. 3 (1984): 265–291; and "From the Truman Doctrine to the Second Superpower Detente: The Rise and Fall of the Cold War," *Journal of Peace Research* 27, no. 1 (1990): 25–42.

4. Ken Booth, *Strategy and Ethnocentrism* (London: Croom Helm, 1979).

5. Richard C. Snyder, H. W. Bruck, Burton M. Sapin, eds., *Foreign Policy Decision-Making: An Approach to the Study of International Politics* (New York: Free Press, 1962).

6. John Vasquez, *The Power of Power Politics: A Critique* (New Brunswick, NJ: Rutgers University Press, 1983).

7. For the main statements of the opposing sides in this "debate," see the essays in K. Knorr and J. Rosenau, eds., *Contending Approaches to International Politics* (Princeton, NJ: Princeton University Press, 1969).

8. See, for example, James N. Rosenau, "Puzzlement in Foreign Policy," *Jerusalem Journal of International Relations* 1, no. 4 (1986): 1–10; and his "International Studies in a Transnational World," *Millennium* 5, no. 1 (1976): 1–20.

9. For this claim, see James N. Rosenau, "Restlessness, Change and Foreign Policy Analysis," in Rosenau, ed., *In Search of Global Patterns* (New York: Free Press, 1976), pp. 369–376; and also his "Comparative Foreign Policy: One-time Fad, Realized Fantasy, and Normal Field," in C. Kegley, G. Raymond, R. Rood, and R. Skinner, eds., *International Events and the Comparative Analysis of Foreign Policy* (Columbia, SC: University of South Carolina Press, 1975), p. 35.

10. J. David Singer, "The Levels-of-Analysis Problem in International Relations," *World Politics* 14 (October 1961): 77–92.

11. See Anthony Giddens, *The Constitution of Society: Outline of the Theory of Structuration* (Cambridge: Polity Press, 1984).

12. Alex Wendt, "The Agent-Structure Problem in International Relations Theory," *International Organization* 41, no. 3 (1987): 335–370. For this author's views on this topic, see Martin Hollis and Steve Smith, *Explaining and Understanding International Relations* (Oxford: Oxford University Press, 1990). See also our comment on, amongst others, structuration theory in Martin Hollis and Steve Smith, "Beware of Gurus: Structure and Action in International Relations," *Review of International Studies* 17, no. 4 (1991): 393–410.

13. See *Millennium* 17, no. 3 (1988).

14. Robert Cox, "Social Forces, States, and World Order: Beyond International Relations Theory," *Millennium* 10, no. 2 (1981):126–155.

15. See Robert Keohane, "International Relations Theory: Contributions of a Feminist Standpoint," *Millennium* 18, no. 2 (1989): 245–253.

16. Fred Halliday, "States, Discources, Classes: A Rejoinder to Suganami, Forbes and Palan," *Millennium* 17, no. 1 (1988): 77–80.

17. Cynthia Enloe, *Bananas, Beaches and Bases: Making Feminist Sense of International Politics* (London: Pandora Press, 1989).

18. *International Studies Quarterly* 34, no. 3 (September 1990), guest edited by Richard Ashley and R.B.J. Walker.

19. George Friedman and Meredith Lebard, *The Coming War with Japan* (New York, St Martin's Press, 1991).

Act IV

1. See, in particular, Jacques Derrida, *Of Grammatology* (Baltimore, MD: Johns Hopkins University Press, 1977).

2. Jacques Derrida, *The Post Card: From Socrates to Freud and Beyond* (Chicago: Chicago University Press, 1987), p. 52.

3. See "Polemics, Politics, and Problemizations," in P. Rabinow, ed., *The Foucault Reader* (New York: Pantheon Books, 1984), pp. 381–382.

4. For a fuller understanding of how identity is not internally but dialogically constructed in a verbal community, see Mikhail Bakhtin, *The Dialogic Imagination: Four Essays by M. M. Bakhtin*, ed. Michael Holquist (Austin: University of Texas Press, 1981); Tzvetan Todorov, *Mikhail Bakhtin: The Dialogical Principle* (Minneapolis: University of Minnesota Press, 1984); and Paul de Man, "Dialogue and Dialogism," in *The Resistance to Theory* (Minneapolis: University of Minnesota Press, 1986).

5. Mikhail Bakhtin, *Marxism and the Philosophy of Language* (New York: Seminar Press, 1973), p. 39.

6. See William Connolly, *Identity\Difference: Democratic Negotiation of Political Paradox* (Ithaca and London: Cornell University Press, 1991), for an incisive study of the impact of the "globalization of contingency" on public identities.

7. Mikhail Bakhtin, *Problems of Dostoevsky's Poetics*, trans. Caryl Emerson (Minneapolis: University of Minnesota Press, 1984), p. 318.

8. Mikhail Bakhtin, "Concerning Methodology in the Human Sciences," quoted by Todorov in *Dialogical Principle*, p. 110.

9. This has been an ongoing project, crudely begun in "Hedley Bull and the Idea of a Diplomatic Culture," a paper presented at the annual meeting of the British International Studies Association, 1986; outlined in an introductory essay, "The Boundaries of Knowledge and Power in International Relations," in James Der Derian and Michael Shapiro, eds., *International/Intertextual Relations: Postmodern Readings of World Politics* (Lexington, MA: Lexington Press, 1989), pp. 3–10; and completed in my book, *Antidiplomacy: Spies, Terror, Speed, and War in International Relations* (Oxford: Basil Blackwell, 1992). The dialogical approach has also been adroitly applied to IR by Richard Ashley in his essay, "Living on Border Lines: Man, Poststructuralism, and War," in Der Derian and Shapiro, eds., *International/Intertextual Relations,* pp. 259–322. And R.B.J. Walker has convincingly taken apart the "inside/outside" dichotomy upon which much of IR rests in *Inside/Outside: International Politics as Political Theory* (Cambridge: Cambridge University Press, 1993).

10. De Man, "Dialogue and Dialogism," p. 109.

11. On the appeal of "heroic theory" and "sovereign voices" in IR, see Richard Ashley, "Untying the Sovereign State: A Double Reading of the Anarchy Problematique," *Millennium Journal of International Studies* 17, no. 2 (Summer 1988): 227–262; and Richard Ashley, "Living on Border Lines: Man, Poststructuralism, and War," in James Der Derian and Michael Shapiro, eds., *International/Intertextual Relations: Postmodern Readings of World Politics* (Lexington, MA: Lexington Press, 1989), pp. 259–321.

12. Nancy Huston makes this point in another context, of the exclusion of women from the making of war and war narrative. See "Tales of War and Tears of Women," *Women Studies International Forum* 5, no. 3/4 (1982): 271.

13. For example, Robert Keohane's view that the "postmodern project is a dead-end in the study of international relations—and that it would be disastrous for feminist international relations theory to pursue this path." See "International Relations Theory: Contributions of a Feminist Standpoint," *Millennium* (Summer 1989): 249.

14. On the debate between "French" and "American" varieties of feminism, see, for example, Toril Moi, "Feminism, Postmodernism, and Style: Recent Feminist Criticism in the United States," *Cultural Critique* (Spring 1988): 3–22. On the introduction of feminist theory into IR, see *Millennium* (Winter 1988), a special issue on women in international relations; V. Spike Peterson and Jane Jaquette, conference report, "Clarification and Contestation: Woman, the State and War: What Difference Does Gender Make?" Occasional Paper, Center for International Studies, University of Southern California, Los Angeles, 1989; and Christine Sylvester, "Reconstituting a Gender Eclipsed Dialogue" (Act II of this volume).

15. The remarkable exception is Tzvetan Todorov's *The Conquest of America*, trans. R. Howard (New York: Harper and Row, 1984).

16. From the "real" Mother Courage, just before she sings "The Song of the Great Capitulation." See Bertolt Brecht, *Mother Courage and Her Children*, trans. Eric Bentley (New York: Grove Press, 1963), p. 67.

17. *New York Times,* February 22, 1990.

18. *Congressional Record*, February 22, 1990. Perhaps this helps us to better understand why Havel met with Frank Zappa in Prague before he met with political scientists at Georgetown University.

19. Timothy Garton Ash, "The Revolution of the Magic Lantern," *New York Review of Books,* January 18, 1990, p. 42.

20. See P. Virilio, *Bunker Archeologie* (Paris: Centre de Creation Industrielle, 1975); *L'Insecurite du Territoire* (Paris: Galilee, 1977); *Vitesse et Politique* (Paris: Galilee, 1978) *Speed and Politics: An Essay on Dromology,* trans. M. Polizzotti (New York: Semiotext[e], 1986); *Defense Populaire et Luttes Ecologiques* (Paris: Galilee, 1978); *Esthetique de la Disparition* (Paris: Balland, 1980); *Pure War* (New York: Semiotext[e], 1983); *Guerre et Cinema: Logistique de la Perception* (Paris: Editions de l'Etoile, 1984); *L'espace Critique* (Paris: Christian Bourgeois, 1984); *L'horizon Negatif* (Paris: Galilee, 1984); and *La Machine de Vision* (Paris: Editions Galilee, 1988).

21. P. Virilio, *Pure War,* p. 115.

22. *New York Times,* March 30, 1990.

23. Adam Michnik, "Notes on the Revolution," *New York Times Magazine,* March 11, 1990, p. 44.

Act V

1. As 1960s alums will recognize instantly, this title is a direct appropriation of the title of one of Bob Dylan's albums.

2. See Albert Camus, *Resistance, Rebellion and Death* (New York: Knopf, 1961) and *The Rebel* (New York: Vintage Books, 1956).

3. The criteria come from Jean Bethke Elshtain, "Feminist Political Rhetoric and Women's Studies," in John S. Nelson, Allan Megill and Donald N. McCloskey, eds., *The Rhetoric of the Human Sciences: Language and Argument in Scholarship and Public Affairs* (Madison: University of Wisconsin Press, 1987), pp. 319–340.

4. Alan Ryan, "A Society of Nations?" *Times Literary Supplement,* March 22, 1991, p. 5.

5. Hannah Arendt, *On Violence* (New York: Harvest/HBJ, 1969). The discussion of Arendt, including footnoted material, is drawn directly from Jean Bethke Elshtain, "Realism, Just War and Feminism in a Nuclear Age," *Political Theory* 13, no. 1 (February 1985): 39–57.

6. Arendt, *On Violence,* p. 5.

7. Kenneth N. Waltz, *Man, the State and War* (New York: Columbia University Press, 1959).

8. See Jean Bethke Elshtain, *Women and War* (New York: Basic Books, 1987) and my essay, "The Problem with Peace," *Millennium* 17, no. 3 (Winter 1988): 441–451.

9. See V. Spike Peterson and Jane Jaquette, conference report, "Clarification and Contestation: Woman, the State and War: What Difference Does Gender Make?" Occasional Paper, Center for International Studies, University of Southern California, Los Angeles, California, 1989, p. 17, where I put these questions during the course of a discussion.

10. I am drawing variously on reading Taylor over the years. Check out Charles Taylor, *Philosophical Papers,* vols. 1 and 2 (Cambridge: Cambridge University Press, 1985).

11. See Benedict Anderson, *Imagined Communities: Reflections on the Origin and Spread of Nationalism* (London: Verso, 1983).

12. See my essay, "Sovereign, Identity and Sacrifice," which exists in three versions: *Social Research* 58, no. 3 (Fall 1991): 545–562; *Millennium* 20, no. 3 (Winter 1991): 395–406; and in V. Spike Peterson, ed., *Gendered States: Feminist (Re)visions of IR Theory* (Boulder: Lynne Rienner, 1992).

13. Daniel Garst, "Thucydides and Neorealism," *International Studies Quarterly* 33, no. 1 (March 1989): 3–28; and James H. Nolt, "Social Order and War: Thucydides, Aristotle, and the Critique of Modern Realism," unpublished manuscript presented at the annual meeting of the American Political Science Association, 1989.

14. Joan Wallach Scott, *Gender and the Politics of History* (New York: Columbia University Press, 1988), p. 7.

15. Jane Jaquette, "Machiavelli," unpublished manuscript, pp. 2, 4, 5.

16. See Jean Bethke Elshtain, "Sovereign God, Sovereign State, Sovereign Self," *Notre Dame Law Review* 66, no. 5 (1991): 1355–1378; and Mona Harrington, "What Exactly Is Wrong with the Liberal State as an Agent of Feminist Change?" in Peterson, ed., *Gendered States.*

17. The wonderful words in quotes belong to Isaiah Berlin, "Two Concepts of Nationalism: An Interview with Isaiah Berlin," *New York Review of Books,* November 21, 1991, pp. 19–23.

18. "Home" appears in the *New York Review of Books,* December 5, 1991, p. 49.

Epilogue

1. The ensuing six paragraphs are from a letter to James N. Rosenau from Christine Sylvester dated May 18, 1992.

2. Ole R. Holsti and James N. Rosenau, "The Foreign Policy Beliefs of Women in Leadership Positions," *Journal of Politics* 43 (May 1981): 326–347.

3. James N. Rosenau, *Turbulence in World Politics* (Princeton: Princeton University Press, 1990).

About the Book and Editor

Who *are* these characters—Westfem and SAR, Tsitsi and SUKA, Mother Courage, SICC, and GORP—and what do they have to say about the state of contemporary international affairs? For a painless yet provocative introduction to some of the most ponderous issues in world politics today, consider this book of dialogues written by leading lights in international relations research, covering everything from the New World Order to the role of postmodernism in constructing an answer to the deconstruction of the Soviet Union.

Global Voices develops as five different "dialoguers" spin out exchanges between and among such protagonists as the archetypal Senior American Researcher, his British and feminist counterparts, a thoughtful young Western feminist, her Third World alter ego, a concerned (but skeptical) citizen, and a set of postmodern personae as elusive as quicksilver. Youth and age, male and female, realist and idealist, science and art, Western and Third World—all find their voices represented here.

Between the scenes, the characters' defenses come down along with the Berlin Wall, and the dialogues unravel in tandem with American hegemony, the Soviet republics, and gender-bound visions of "reality." This entertaining survey of issues, theory, and controversy in international relations is appropriate for readers both inside and outside the discipline, and is perfect for students who want to "listen in" on conversations that are reshaping the contours of international political thought as well as action.

James N. Rosenau is University Professor of International Affairs at George Washington University. He is the author or editor of numerous publications, including *The United Nations in a Turbulent World, Governance without Government,* and *Turbulence in World Politics: A Theory of Change and Continuity.*

About the Contributors

James Der Derian is associate professor of international relations at the University of Massachusetts at Amherst. He is author of *On Diplomacy: Genealogy of Western Diplomacy* and, most recently, *Antidiplomacy: Spies, Terror, Speed, and War in International Politics.*

Jean Bethke Elshtain is Centennial Professor of Political Science and professor of philosophy at Vanderbilt University. She is the author of numerous publications, including *Public Man, Private Woman: Women in Social and Political Thought, Women and War,* and *Power Trips and Other Journeys.*

Steve Smith is professor of international politics at the University of Wales, Aberystwyth. He has taught international relations (and regularly attended conferences) on both sides of the Atlantic. Editor of the Cambridge University Press Series in International Relations, he recently coauthored *Explaining and Understanding International Relations.*

Christine Sylvester is associate professor of political science at Northern Arizona University. She is author of *Feminist Theory and International Relations Theory in a Post-Modern Era* and *Zimbabwe: The Terrain of Contradictory Development.*